Holding Space

How To Help Women Feel Safe

Holding Space

How To Help Women Feel Safe

Leslie Karen Hammond

Pueblo Press

Holding Space

By Leslie Karen Hammond

Front cover photo: Pixabay Interior images from Pixabay and Leslie Karen Hammond

Published by:
Pueblo Press
677 Cash Street, Croydon, NH 03773

Interior Design by Mark Roberts, Croatan Press

Requests for permission from:
Global Wisdom
860-303-8772

ISBN: 978-0-9836344-8-5

Other Books By Leslie Karen Hammond:

Tap Your Source

Women Rising; How To Go From Uncomfortable To Unstoppable

Keep It Real; Why We're Afraid To Speak Up and What To Do About It

Find us on social media:

Healing Through Your Story

Healing Through Your Story

Leslie Karen Hammond

Stories Impact

@ConfidenceBldr

Leslie Karen Hammond

Dedication

The manifestation of a dream begins with first with a vision, second with the moral and often financial support of family, and lastly with someone who can get you in an ideal situation that allows you to test your knowledge and skillset.

Getting to the destination takes a village, staying takes heart. Once put into a new environment, it's up to the individual to inspire the people they came to reach. Many people played a part in making the experiences in this book possible, far too many to list individually.

Holding Space is dedicated to every woman who senses she has greatness within but no one to draw it out of her, and to my two favorite men.

To my son, Josh, thank you for supporting the work that fills my soul when at times the risks I take make no sense - I love you for who you have helped me become. Instead of a mother to only you, I am becoming a mother to thousands.

To my husband, Itancan Wasaka, thank you for all you do to support the journey into what I'm capable of accomplishing. Every time you got more excited than me at each opportunity I had to travel and stretch my skills, I felt valued and loved. You've always known I was destined for global work; I'm grateful you consistently hold the space for me to make my contribution to the world becoming a better place for all women.

To the remainder of my family, friends, and clients - THANK YOU for the depth of our exchanges. You taught me some of the most valuable lessons that prepared me for serving a broader audience.

Contents

Acknowledgments

A special thanks to Jerrie Ueberle, thank you for taking a chance on me and trusting my experience to be of value to the members of the World Academy for the Future of Women (WAFW). I appreciate the way you remind me to be an example for women globally.

To the WAFW members in China from Sias International University, the members in Nepal from Orchid International College and Imadol Cultural Learning Center, and the members from University of Liberal Arts Bangladesh - thank you for being the inspiration for this book! You opened your heart to let me in and gave me a new understanding of the world and how I fit into it.

To the Boards of Director, Administration, and Faculty of each institute of learning that sponsored us, thank you for opening your doors for WAFW. I've learned so much about advancing and accelerating women's leadership worldwide from your willingness to support a global initiative.

To all the facilitators I've met along the way from different backgrounds, countries, and continents – it's been a pleasure to inspire women around the world with you. Thank you!

From the outside, travel for WAFW looks adventurous and perhaps exotic. There is more that happens behind the scenes to make these experiences possible than you can imagine. Danielle Hampson and Tess Mosko Scherer - Thank You for all you contributed either technically or in moral support.

The day to day operations of each WAFW is the responsibility of the leadership team in each location. Women often with no or little leadership time under their belts, volunteer to step into a realm where they have no experience.

Consider for a moment women in cultures who historically are looked down upon when unmarried, told they're fortunate to get educated, and expected to be compliant. Now imagine the handful of women who in spite of cultural norms dare to step forward to lead.

While launching new academies in Nepal and Bangladesh, I had a combination of teams. In Nepal, there were a few alumni from the previous year in Imadol. In Bangladesh, women, and men who knew little about the academy but believed in the mission, came together because they wanted to improve the conditions for women in their country.

The success we experienced during the initial stages of recruitment, wasn't possible without all of their assistance. Start-up teams, THANK YOU!

Regardless of how established, an academy is in any country, expansion across new borders brings unforeseen circumstances. Having had the opportunity to help WAFW enter a new location in Nepal and begin in Bangladesh in 2018, I've learned the importance of weaving Western ideas and Eastern paradigms.

It's important to acknowledge the diplomacy it takes on both sides to achieve a mutually desired outcome in spite of the speed bumps.

Everyone begins with a particular vision, then finds common ground.

Preparing for the role of WAFW Start-Up Coordinator took every leadership role, every success, and failure I've had in life. At times my heart led the charge, in other moments strategy had the wheel. In any occasion where my ego got ruffled, I had to remember the higher purpose and move to that end.

Preface

While sitting in my first coaching circle of forty college-age women, in Dhaka, Bangladesh, for the first time in twenty years, I felt helpless.

As their facilitator, I'm the one they trust to inspire them. In all the coaching circles I've sat in between China and Nepal, nothing as intense as the emotion in this circle has ever happened.

My business is empowering women; I'm supposed to have the appropriate questions to provoke a woman to find her answers within. On this day, in this group, a few words rolled off my tongue with the intent to soothe the violated, wounded women, who found the courage to share.

Whatever that sentence or two was, it felt incredibly inadequate considering the magnitude of what just got shared. Being at a loss for words rarely happens to me these days, but a variety of circumstances contributed to the perfect storm of shock and awe, all I could do was listen.

Fast forward a few hours, it's 12:20 am. I ought to be sleeping. The antihistamine isn't working to induce drowsiness; I'm listening to a meditation soundtrack, and all my heart wants to do is empty my mind of the memories from October 20th into my computer, so I don't lose them.

Amid extreme exhaustion from the last four weeks of intense recruitment first in Nepal and now in Dhaka, the physical and emotional depletion of doing the job of two full-time people has reached a level, that makes it a struggle to reset. Writing in the middle of the night is the last thing I ought to be doing. But ignoring the resiliency of these women would be an injustice to the generations to follow.

The women of WAFW helped create a new depth of understanding of the human condition for me. The oppression women face in the USA is a luxury compared to the conditions women face globally. I intend to inspire you whether you are a parent, an educator, a mentor or an activist. Our combined efforts in every home, every school, every workplace, and in every country influence the future for generations to come. But before fixing what's outside, people need to look inside.

Holding Space also represents the potential of the human spirit. If I can manifest a life of travel and global influence on a shoestring, you can too. By no means do I have a large bank account (nor a credit card), I'm always trusting the money will show up to pay bills. One can spend their life dreaming or living a dream. Aspiring to do anything more extensive than serving one's self, especially when it's to be of service to others, creates incredible opportunities beyond your imagination.

The momentum life took on after first the first of many YESES, began with volunteering for WAFW China in September 2017. The experience is nothing short of extraordinary. Since the alignment of the academy's mission is so near to mine, I've taken financial risks some consider crazy, to remain connected and share my perspectives on leadership, life and what it takes to find the unstoppable woman within.

May these pages inspire you to live boldly and trust you are here for a reason - to leave humanity stronger than when you arrived and feel fulfilled in the process.

Introduction

Holding Space describes what I've observed over eight months in Asia from September 2017 through February 2019. My time got spent with college-age women in China, Nepal, and Bangladesh who found the courage to join, World Academy for the Future of Women, a global leadership training organization.

The striking similarities found across cultural divides and beyond age were remarkable. It was as though I saw myself in earlier years before the clarity of purpose got revealed. Additionally, the women's willingness to open their hearts further reinforced the calling I followed for the last twenty years; empowering women to find their voice and use it.

Expect to dive into the psyche of not just women, but also paradigms of the human condition as I've had the privilege to witness.

Lastly, if you're tired of saying you want to make a difference in the world and are willing to accept an invitation to begin, you'll read about what it's like to walk in the shoes of a facilitator for WAFW from my experience. There are always opportunities for you to begin serving on a broader scale.

With each page, I trust you'll get transported into a state of reflection, possibility, and inspiration.

"Insanity is doing the same thing over again and expecting different results."

\- *Albert Einstein*

Chapter 1

Helpless Versus Hopeless

When was the last time you watched or listened to a story that left you so desperately wanting to say something to ease another person's pain, and you couldn't find the words?

That was me three nights ago.

Most people find it difficult to tolerate another person in emotional distress. Due to the observer's discomfort, or empathic nature, there's a primal need to alleviate suffering. The way people handle any stressful emotional circumstance is as unique as the individual. Those who assist best often seek career paths that compliment their skill. Some empathize, others use humor, and there are the occasional folks who convince you it's all your own doing.

I've developed a great admiration for professionals who facilitate support groups for those in continuing turmoil. It's challenging to bear witness to someone who complains about their situation with no desire to make progress.

Most women in the World Academy for the Future of Women (WAFW) have a desire to create change in their lives. What they lack in many cases is clear direction and the support of culture, family, or colleagues.

WAFW offers tools for women to discover their direction and the support of other women with the same desire to know their passion and purpose. The initial stages of growth are remarkable for those ready. Women are hungry for equality and opportunity.

Sixteen months ago I was introduced to the World Academy for the Future of Women (WAFW). An organization started in 2009 by Jerrie Ueberle. A woman of vision, wisdom and, tenacity, she is changing the way women live and lead. “A bold and daring leadership program” is how the Academy gets described to candidates for membership, volunteers, and philanthropists. True to its marketing, the program delivers its promise. The WAFW has a track record of success as it moves into its tenth year.

WORLD ACADEMY
FOR THE FUTURE OF WOMEN

What began in China has spread to Nepal and Bangladesh with more countries in the queue. The goal is to continue expanding into nations where women with the least opportunities for gender equality get the chance to create a future they desire for themselves, their countries, and ultimately transform the world we presently know into a world where we all be proud to live.

In the last year, I've been to China and Nepal twice, Bangladesh once with a return trip to all three countries in the next six months. You could say I'm hooked. The mission of the academy is to empower women so they can bring the much-needed change into the villages of its members. But the work isn't intended for only their communities of origin. The WAFW wants to change countries and ultimately to influence global improvement in the lives of women and children where the United Nations Sustainable Development Goals (SDGs) fall short.

I'm in Dhaka, Bangladesh now, been here for three weeks of a six-week stay. I came here to launch the World Academy with a new partner university. Two weeks before arriving in Dhaka I was in Nepal for the same purpose.

During my spring 2018 trip to Nepal, I got so inspired by the progress of the women in the WAFW I committed to the founder I'd always be part of the organization in some capacity. I soon volunteered to be the startup coordinator when the person who usually did the task wasn't available.

The backstory of what qualifies me to perform this role comes from the numerous women I've worked with over the years. This WAFW experience opened my eyes yet again and invited me to share the countless ways you can "hold space" to help another feel safe. This body of work isn't about me; it is about the women who've trusted me; some from the WAFW and others the universe has united with me.

If you're tired of feeling frustrated, do something different. If the uncomfortable situations you encounter repeat themselves, consider other options. It's a lot easier to complain than to make a conscious choice to change something and stick with it. Helplessness and hopelessness are states of mind based on circumstance. When one can see a situation in its most basic form without emotion or a long backstory, there's a far better chance of transforming anything.

One of the operating principles of the World Academy going through my mind is, "reasons don't equal results." The debate on the distinction between a reason and an excuse regularly occurs in my mind. Sometimes I hear the echo of a teenager desperately rationalizing a so-called "good reason" to make the lack of common sense or experience appear as a valid excuse for misbehavior.

Can you imagine the light bulb moment when a woman realizes what she's capable of accomplishing? There's a particular sparkle in the eye, and a significant energetic shift one can feel. It's unmistakable. It's magical. It's inspiring.

Before the epiphany of possibility comes the awareness of responsibility. No one enjoys the recognition of an action which set into motion a series of events that changes the course of one's life into more challenging territory. Once a woman sees what happened, it's critical to find the lesson and not allow her to dwell in the negativity.

Many cultures live in fear and people have an intimate relationship with the adverse circumstances of their lives. Almost out of duty, each generation needs to pass on the mindset of how a woman is supposed to think, behave, and live. Poverty can shape the soul into trusting all one needs gets provided, or all is destined to be a struggle.

With multiple generations or joint families living under the same roof or nearby, there's no escape from the constant reminder of how a woman is supposed to be. Let's rephrase that; the moments a woman can physically remove herself from the weight of a suppressive environment are few. However, the opportunities a woman can remove herself intellectually and emotionally get dictated by the support she receives. Daydreaming is free.

In the Asian cultures I've facilitated within, women are rarely alone. Daughters become the confidants of mothers when there are no other women in the household. Women seem always to travel or live in numbers. Finding a quiet room is often relegated to the washroom. If a woman wants to sit in quiet contemplation, she frequently gets asked what's bothering her.

Some women in a household are hypersensitive to the emotional well-being of the other women, much like women's menstrual cycles will align with one another. Therefore, when a mother, grandmother, auntie, cousin or sister clings to insecurity, unworthiness, or fear everything she sees, hears, says, and does come through the lens of her reality. It takes a determined woman to overcome the emotional adversity of a culture or a family when she trusts there is a broader future for herself.

The only salve for the emotional onslaught of negativity is trusting in the possibility for one's self. Although women in Asia bear these conditions more intensely than most North American women, you don't need to look far to recognize the similarities in your community. When does enough become enough?

In spite of the challenges, a few women I met have supportive families. Some study abroad and return to their country of origin to exercise what they know and shift their destiny from marriage to career: not all, but some.

So on a Saturday like almost any other, in a university classroom in Dhaka, forty women sat in a circle for a coaching session. The number is significant because it's many more women than we usually have or prefer for that matter. Coaching is intended to be conducted in small intimate groups to give enough physical and energetic space for women to feel safe enough to share something troubling them or a challenge inside or outside of the WAFW. The coaching space is for whatever the women need. This session the women needed to be heard.

Halfway through, one woman shared her story of sexual abuse. Then another. Then another until five women found the courage to stop stifling the anger, shame, and isolation. In a Muslim country, it's not only unusual for a woman to share their story of such treatment, in many cases it's dangerous. For starters, she gets blamed for the offense against her. Many times she is shamed further. If the former doesn't occur, then she is shushed and dismissed.

The most surprising thing about this coaching circle was the level of trust and safety these women created within the four walls of classroom 405. These women showed and felt empathy in a new way for one another. Most importantly, the women who spoke up realized they were not alone. Through the tears, the rage, and the relief their sharing brought, a calm got created. It was before I recognized the shift from frustration to peace that the inadequacy fueled by my ego, came through.

The voice in my mind shouted, "You're a healer for crying out loud, SAY SOMETHING USEFUL!" It was in the moment of speechlessness I realized, sometimes all you need to do is be attentive with your ears, heart and, eyes - not your mouth.

My lesson from that Saturday coaching session and the inspiration for this book is; many times all you need to do is hold space for others.

You don't need to respond verbally to everything you hear. You don't necessarily need to DO anything to fix the problem. Sometimes all you need to do is create and hold a safe space for things to unfold. Leave your ego and expectations at the door. Leave your need to be right. Leave your impulse to judge behind. Bring your heart, collect your restraint and, open your ears. The universe will see to it you contribute in a way that's needed. Trust you’ll know what to do. Believe you have the skills to navigate the unexpected. Just hold space.

Transforming helplessness and hopelessness into possibility is more likely when there’s an adequate support system. Eventually, a supported woman turns possibility into probability.

Optional Mantras

I belong wherever I find the courage to go.

I trust God/the Universe explicitly.

I have the power to change my mind anytime I choose.

"Getting over a painful experience is much like crossing the monkey bars. You have to let go at some point in order to move forward."

– C.S. Lewis

Chapter 2

Hope Less, Trust More

I hope… When you hope for something, how much attention do you honestly put on your aspiration after the words leave you? Five seconds? Ten seconds?

Call me a cynic, but hope feels like a word people use with good intentions but unconsciously dismiss almost immediately. When at a loss for words, "I hope you…" is the most sincere reply many can muster to a variety of disturbing news people share.

Folks mean well, but I question the effectiveness of making this statement.

Instead of hoping, imagine the confidence boost you'd give someone by saying to them, "I trust you've got this!"

Are you willing to give a quick experiment a go? Let's say you, and I are having tea. You tell me about a challenge you're experiencing in your family. You're sitting across the table from me feeling defeated, exhausted and at the end of your patience. I look you straight in the eyes and say, "I hope you get through this soon." The tone of my voice may be soft, nurturing or even doubtful based on what you tell me. How reassured will you feel? Now imagine I look at you and say, "I trust you'll find a way through this quickly and whatever happens, it will be the best thing for you (or your family) right now." Can you imagine how different the tone of my voice might sound? Will you be more reassured?

Hope is soft. Hope leaves too many uncertainties. Hope is the easy way out.

Trust on the other hand sends a deliberate message to the universe that you are serious about fixing whatever you're experiencing. Trust implies you know a resolution is ahead and you aren't about to quit. Trust suggests action is about to be taken.

Can you envision a world where people make choices out of curiosity instead of abstaining from deciding on anything due to fear? Millions of life-altering moments get lost every day because people cannot believe they can choose effectively. Fear has an insatiable hunger.

To “hope” less, consider trusting more. Tempting as it is to write you *NEED* to “trust” more, it occurs to me the statement becomes disempowering. Let me be clear on the distinction. The energy behind your words is significantly different when you need something versus when you want something. To declare the need for anything sounds like a plea from a place of vulnerability, not that such transparency is a bad thing, but it's not as empowering as declaring what you want.

Don’t take this writer’s word for it, try an experiment with someone and test the theory yourself. Ask two different people for something and notice how you feel and how your voice sounds with a request from the perspective or need and want.

When asking for anything based on need, it seems to require justification. By the time you finish a potentially long story, you may get what you desire but not through another person's natural desire to give or grant you anything. The request from a place of need creates more of manipulative exchange. Getting what you want under such circumstances can leave another person feeling as though you got one over on them instead of empowering them to give.

Anytime I ask how often women *don't ask* for something because they believe the answer will be NO, a roomful of hands goes up.

Just as fear steals from courage, not asking out of fear, robs the person you want something from of the opportunity to say YES. By not asking, you're taking their chance to surprise you. No promises are getting made you'll get a YES every time, but the more often you ask, the more comfortable you'll get asking for anything. On a parallel note, please stop wishing for things! Making a wish is akin to hoping and unlikely to produce the result you desire.

Ask yourself, do you want a future filled with feelings of inadequacy or the conviction of empowerment? It seems to me everyone can feel inadequate without help. The lingering wounds from past disappointment can wreak havoc on a fragile ego. When you merely hope to "feel" better, you're delaying the recovery process. Trusting the ability to move forward expedites the process.

What appears to be a harmless play on words has an enormous influence on the subconscious. Thoughts reinforce actions. Actions are what creates the future you want. What's the harm in changing your perspective on how you use a few words if the shift can expedite what you desire?

One more empowering distinction in words is the difference between "can't," and "won't." Claiming you can't do something you don't want to is the easy way out. Declaring you won't do something is taking a stand for what you trust to be true or best for you.

Here's an exercise to check your readiness for transitioning from "need to want" and "hope to trust."

Make a list of all the things you hope will happen in the next six months.

1.

2.

3.

4.

5.

6.

Now make a list of things you trust will happen in the next six months.

1.

2.

3.

4.

5.

6.

Which list do you feel more committed to; the hope list or the trust list?

What is provoking your feelings?

On which list are you more naturally committed to getting the results? Consider exploring why that is.

Still not convinced? The next time you hear someone say, "I hope..." for anything in their life, consider politely asking them how they plan to make their desire a reality. Be respectful.

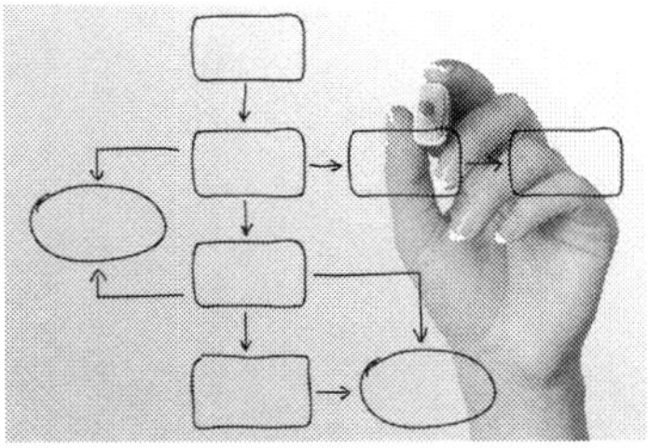

If they look at you like you have two heads, tell them you're experimenting with language and curious how they think. Some folks will gladly play along, others not so much but either way, the discovery will shed light on the character of those you spend time with and trust.

Trust Isn't A Goal, It's A Process

"It is always our own self that we find at the end of the journey. The sooner we face that self, the better."

– Ella Maillart

Chapter 3

Changing The Question

In the presence of anyone facing a challenge, if you're the slightest bit empathic, it's human nature to want to help. However, what most don't realize is the lens through which assumptions get made as to how another person wants help. The world as it occurs to you isn't as it appears to everyone else.

How many times have you thought you knew what someone else wanted or needed and been wrong? Have you ever offended another person in the attempt to assist?

To master the skillset of helping another feel safe, you must first examine your behavior when things go awry. Your reactions to the following questions will dictate how you offer comfort to another.

When you are disappointed, what the first thing you ask of yourself or another?

- Why is this happening to me?
- What did I do to deserve to this?
- Am I ever going to have something good or nice happen to me?

Or do you make statements such as:

- I knew I couldn't trust this person
- I had a bad feeling about that anyway
- Oh well, just one more thing in a string of bad luck

If you related to any of the comments, take a

breath and forgive yourself. Along the journey of your emotional, mental, and psychological evolution as a human being, it was likely necessary to go through a phase of such questions.

Here's a different way to look at things. I'm not implying that particular phase in life was right or wrong, good or bad. I'm not advocating any other idea is better or worse, I'm asking you to look at disappointment from a DIFFERENT perspective.

Imagine instead of asking a question that most likely will provoke a negative answer, what if you could ask:

- How can I learn from this experience?
- What else does my body, mind, or spirit need now that I previously ignored?
- What other opportunity has this created?

Imagine making statements like:

- THANK YOU, Universe for giving me some much needed time for me.
- I'm not taking this disappointment personally. Everyone has a private struggle that can create havoc; I'm in no position to judge.
- What a relief, that event wasn't for my highest good.

Can you sense the energetic shift? It's important to realize how you respond to understand how you will sooth another. It's instinctive to fall back on what you know intimately.

While traveling, it has become increasingly clear how impactful the influence of others is in a moment of crisis. More often than not, I've heard women sharing a fear-based response from those closest to them when they sought support in a traumatic situation.

My observation got based on the stories I heard women sharing in the classroom. Mothers, fathers, aunts, uncles, grandparents, and cousins have a genuine belief they are acting in the best interest of their daughter, niece, granddaughter, etc.

As a mother, I did everything in my power to protect my son from pain and suffering. In hindsight, I now see how much of a disservice to him it was. It's one thing to read a book on parenting and another when in the moment of crisis to know how to respond effectively.

The point here is:

- Not everyone responds the same way you do.
- Sometimes people only need you to listen, not solve their problem.
- No matter how well you know a person, don't assume you know what they want.

What if you approached a person in crisis or better yet, before an emergency and asked them what they *wanted* to feel better? Such a simple idea that creates a potentially awkward conversation.

The intent is to get to know someone close to you on a deeper emotional level to understand better how to help them. Your next question is probably, "How the heck does get this conversation started?!"

One of the best online, free tools I've seen is https://www.5lovelanguages.com/profile/

Knowing how you want to be loved directly reflects on how you show affection and assist others. For example, my primary love language is Acts of Service. When someone does something meaningful for me that I don't ask for, it shows me two things:

1. They care enough to know what I want or find useful

2. They care enough to do something without getting asked

You may not get your friends and family to agree to take the quiz, but if you know yourself better, that's a fantastic start. If you cannot get someone to go online and fill out the brief survey, then look at the questions and ask them casually during a conversation. You'll notice the different love languages by the nature of the people's responses.

To get you started, the five languages are:

- Acts of Service
- Words of Affirmation
- Physical Contact
- Receiving Gifts
- Quality Time

Regardless of whether or not you know the love languages of those closest to you, there's another way to get proactive in support those you care for the most. Once again, it involves asking questions.

Most people regardless of how much personal

transformation work they've done over the years can get unhinged, unglued, or triggered when something strikes them at the core of an unresolved issue. No matter how well you know someone, there will always be unshared secrets.

You cannot force another to tell you the root of their deepest fears, but you can help them feel safe enough to come to you in a moment of need.

One simple act of caring that goes a long way to creating emotional intimacy is asking them what they want. It seems like most women get asked this question about material things but not matters of the heart or with the type of support they most desire.

Earlier you read questions around dealing with disappointment. There are so many ways people can hurt one another, that to name them all would be tedious. Therefore, from what I've seen, here is a summary of the three most significant acts that can shake someone to the core:

- Betrayal
- Failure
- Disrespect

Let's take another look at the questions from how you examine disappointment and see what applies to each of these potentially painful acts.

- How can I learn from this experience?
- What else does my body, mind, or spirit need now that I previously ignored?
- What other opportunity has this created? In your opinion, are these questions all relevant? To me they are, and I'll add one more:
- Is this a pattern?

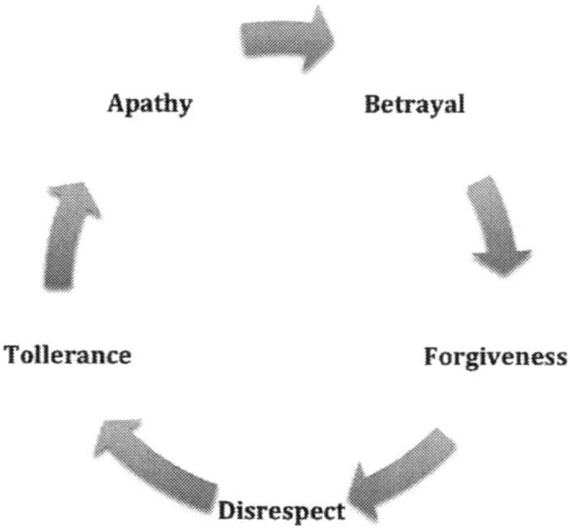

The last question is probably the least pleasant to answer but the most crucial in creating the future you want. Let's be clear about something; it's not your job to point out a pattern in someone else. Bringing such a thing to another person's attention may appear judgmental, and won't likely enhance the relationship. Instead, you're likely to encourage defensiveness and reaction instead of active listening.

What happens when you answer YES to, "Is this a pattern?" More questions. Perhaps not what you wanted to read, but asking more is necessary to start the process of breaking the pattern.

When I notice repeat behavior, I ask:

- When was the last time this happened?
- How did I react to the previous situation?
- When was the time before the last event that this happened?
- Did I behave the same way then?
- When do I recall this situation occurring for the first time?
- How do I feel now that I've noticed a reoccurring pattern?
- What can I do to begin forgiving myself?
- Am I willing to change this pattern?
- If not, what scares me the most?
- What can I do about this fear?
- Who do I trust the most to help me with this?
- If I am willing to change the pattern, what scares me the most?
- What can I do about this fear?
- Who do I trust the most to help me with this?

If you're willing to play along, here's an opportunity to get to know ***you*** through the reflective questions listed.

You're about to take a deep dive into what makes you tick. It's not a good or bad thing if you're not in a mental or emotional position to explore. You can do a little and come back to it later. Skip this exercise if you're not ready, or do it on another piece of paper. It's worth the investment of time and emotion, your return is perspective.

If you find the courage to explore the answers, I promise you'll begin the process of creating healthy boundaries for you and realizing how you can support others. The more stable you are, the clearer you can listen to another and help them without adding your drama to the assistance. Let's begin with:

Betrayal

When was the last time you experienced a betrayal?

____

How did you react?

When was the time before the last event that you felt betrayed?

Did you react the same way then?

When do you recall this situation occurring for the first time?

How do you feel now that you've noticed a reoccurring pattern?

What can you do to begin forgiving yourself?

Are you willing to change this pattern?

If not, what scares you the most?

____

What can you do about this fear?

____

Who do you trust the most to help me with this?

____

If you're willing to change the pattern, what scares you the most?

____

What can you do about this fear?

____

Who do you trust the most to help with this?

____

How has this made you a more positive person?

____

____

Now let's go to:

Failure

When was the last time you feel you failed?

____

How did you react?

____

When was the time before the last event that this happened?

____

Did you behave the same way then?

____

When do you recall this situation occurring for the first time?

____

How do you feel now that you've noticed a reoccurring pattern?

____

What can you do to begin forgiving yourself?

____

Are you willing to change this pattern?

____

If not, what scares you the most?

____

What can you do about this fear?

____

Who do you trust the most to help with this?

____

If you are willing to change the pattern, what scares you the most?

____

What can you do about this fear?

____

Who do you trust the most to help you with this?

____

How has this made you a more positive person?

____

____

Now let's go to:

Disrespect

When was the last time you felt disrespected?

____

How did you react?

____

When was the time before the last event that this happened?

____

Did you behave the same way then?

____

When do you recall this situation occurring for the first time?

____

How do you feel now that you've noticed a reoccurring pattern?

____

What can you do to begin forgiving yourself?

____

Are you willing to change this pattern?

____

If not, what scares you the most?

____

What can you do about this fear?

____

Who do you trust the most to help with this?

____

If you are willing to change the pattern, what scares you the most?

What can you do about this fear?

Who do you trust the most to help you with this?

How has this made you a more positive person?

Reflection is one of the three most powerful tools a person can possess. The other two are the ability to trust, and the ability to forgive.

Once you begin the healing process and change the patterns, ***can you imagine*** making the following statements sincerely and moving on with your life?

THANK YOU, Universe for giving me the opportunity to see this situation differently!

I'm not taking this personally. Everyone has a private struggle that can create havoc; I'm in no position to judge.

What a relief, this circumstance wasn't for my highest good.

With so many questions and potentially more emotionally charged answers, the biggest takeaway I'd love for you to have from this chapter is the importance of asking questions. First asking of yourself, then inquiring compassionately to assist those you care for deeply.

"The assumption that seeing is believing makes us susceptible to visual deception."

- Kathleen Hall Jamieson

Chapter 4

Beyond Assumptions

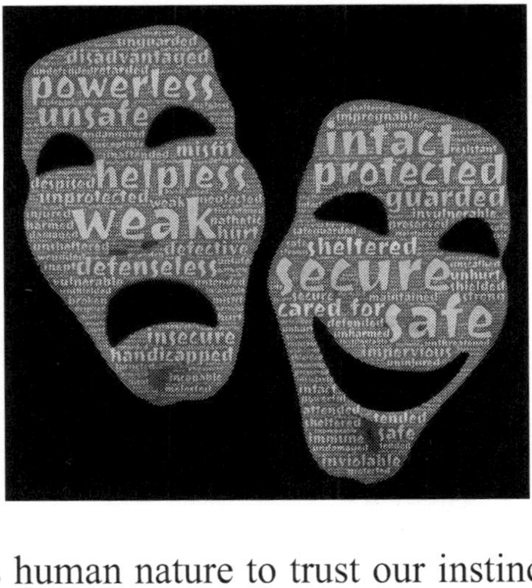

It's human nature to trust our instincts, but how do you discern between what your heart screams, your ego wants, and your gut tells you? How do you know which is the best force to follow? Perhaps the million dollar question. Let's take a look at the differences between each driving force that influences the decisions you make and the way you advise others.

Ah, the heart - the most powerful muscle in the body and the most temperamental. If the chakra system is new for you, basically there are seven energy centers:

- Root Chakra at the base of the tailbone, representing one's sense of stability and security.
- Sacral at the reproductive organs, representing emotions.
- Solar Plexus just below the rib cage, your source of power.
- Heart, love.
- Throat, the ability to express.
- Third Eye in center of the forehead, intuition.
- Crown, above the head, your connection to Source.

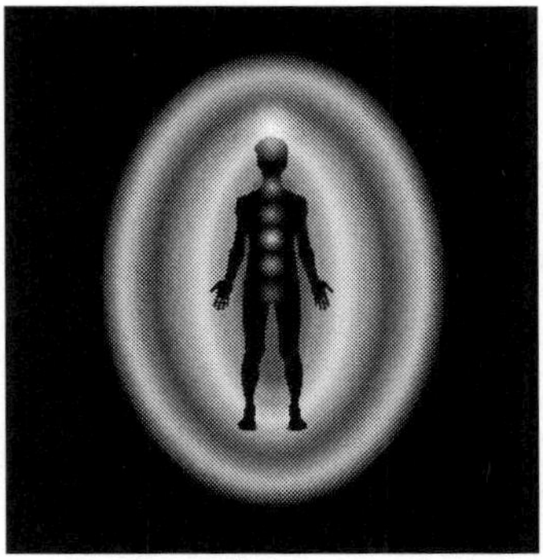

Most folks understand heartache. Filmmakers have depicted crimes of the heart as acts of passion. The negative emotions that stem from matters of the heart range from jealousy to betrayal to hatred. For most, it feels like a debilitating pain that cannot get described to the magnitude one feels. In acts of frustration or despair, the irrational side of a person gets revealed, or true colors come out.

How do you know when your heart is screaming if what you feel is an accurate interpretation of any given situation? The heart and every part of the body for that matter have what's called, muscle memory. Consider it similar to one's ability to ride a bike, once you learn you rarely forget. The heart remembers every pain you've encountered. Unless you've gotten proactive and worked through the issues you were hurt in; your tendency may be to react from the deep seeded pain that remains within you. It doesn't take much to get triggered.

Even when you approach a situation from a place of love, the same trigger can apply, but instead of coming forth negatively it can get expressed through excessive affection. Actions performed through the act of love come from the perspective and experience of the person doing the deed. Someone who craves love can come across either as needy or so giving it can feel smothering.

Let's circle back to how you come to a situation based on what your heart screams. Consider how you have or haven't felt loved in your lifetime. Look at how you've got hurt. What you've experienced shapes your assumptions. Please understand, your history of pain and the level of forgiveness work you've done dictates how you react in every situation. Feeling overwhelmed triggers the emotion of every memory in your life similar to what you directly experience or see someone close to you go through.

The surge of distress makes it easy to assume any misinterpreted behavior is a personal attack. In joyful times, it's easy to turn your back on the discomfort of your life that needs attention to heal. Life seems good; everyone is happy - why open Pandora's Box? To fully understand the value of this chapter, I'm inviting you to notice, to be aware of the influence of the unresolved or unforgiven things in your life. A once broken heart paves the way for assumptions.

Now let's move onto my next favorite topic (tongue in cheek), the ego.

If you've ever seen a cartoon with a little angel on one shoulder of a person and a devil on the other, the ego is the devil. Some describe this segment of the psyche as a necessary piece of a person to drive them to success. It's been my experience that the ego is a troublemaker, a jokester, and an instigator.

Ego insists you are always correct, never humble, and believe it or not in your lowest moments, undeserving of anything pleasant in life. Your ego gets bored quickly and can stir up trouble faster than excrement attracts flies.

Have you noticed how some folks cannot admit they're wrong? Or that some people get offended and take an innocent comment personally? That's the ego at work. It's always interesting how the energy of something you cannot touch or see can wreak so much havoc.

When the hair on the back of your neck goes up, take a breath and ask yourself, "Why am I taking this personally?" It won't be comfortable in the heat of the moment when your emotions are driving your thoughts, words, and actions - but it's possible to switch gears and observe what's happening.

When the need to be "right" surfaces, get curious about why it matters. What difference does it make? If concern over other people's judgment arises, that's a confidence issue. You can spend your life pleasing or impressing others, or you can do what your heart desires. This notion comes from my perspective after decades of diving into personal development work and facing my demons. The idea of following my heart also comes from my calling to be in service to others, not from selfishness. There's a distinct difference between living to get ahead and prove others wrong versus living to give back and make the world a different place.

Your pain, your ego, and your experience show up energetically before your person does. Let me explain. Imagine the vibration or the energy a happy child sends out. You feel great in their presence and cannot help but to smile. Now consider a negative person who complains about everything. How do you feel in their presence? Oftentimes you can feel the negativity coming off an unhappy person without them speaking.

Energy speaks louder than words. Energy travels faster and farther than words. You can feel something odd and not know the source. Therefore, you can send out the vibration of judgment, righteousness, or anger without speaking. There is unmistakable energy about a person who believes they are better than everyone else. When the ego takes the wheel, anyone who disagrees with you can turn into feeling manipulated - like you're getting attacked. You may feel threatened and go into defense mode.

When a person driven by ego observes another person experiencing anything they perceive as an attack from their experience, they may be quick to jump in to defend based on what they feel, hear or see. An assumption often gets made before asking the other person if the interference is wanted.

Ego is like a hungry dog that has its jaws locked on a juicy steak and refuses to let go. Ego only knows survival; nothing else matters. When bored, the ego creates situations to feed. Ego lives to make assumptions. Is it clearer now how this part of the psyche is the troublemaker, a jokester, and an instigator?

Will ego ever go away? No. What can you do to keep it in check? See it coming, acknowledge it, then tell it to ride in the back seat, it doesn't get to drive the car. The next time you make an assumption, ask why you jumped to that conclusion and if being "right" truly matters.

With practice you'll notice more quickly how the heart and ego steer you.

However, awareness doesn't equate mastery. Enter the solar plexus. Perhaps your strongest radar and energy center that speaks the loudest! The solar plexus can throw even the strongest people off balance.

Fear manifests first in the body in the midsection. One can feel something without ever knowing the cause of discomfort. The most important question you can ask yourself when faced with a situation that drives you to nausea is; “Is my life in danger?”

The sensation to fight or flight is real. Ego will drive you to fight for survival or to run for it. The energetic perception of what occurs during the moment of fear gets misinterpreted; emotional safety transforms into a need for physical security.

Look at public speaking, for example, a classic case of emotional havoc immediately inducing physical symptoms. It’s natural to be afraid of the unknown, getting judged by peers, or making a fool of oneself. The misfortune of granting permission to self to back away, to quit or dismiss an opportunity because the outcome is unpredictable is a terrible shame.

Circling back to assumptions, when something scares you it's likely you'll trust everyone else feels the same way you do. It becomes a puzzle as to *WHY or HOW* other people can perform the way they do when to you something feels unfathomable.

Your fears will influence how you advise others, how you attempt to protect others, and how you most importantly how you judge another's behavior. It takes a great deal of practice to see the world through another's eyes or walk in their shoes.

This phenomenon is evident in every family, every relationship, and every country I've visited. Regardless of how safe an activity is, a parent or loved one cannot help themselves in wanting to protect you or anyone else they care about from harm.

When you have a culture that supports fear-based living, it takes generations to adopt a different perspective.

Once the transformation begins to explore different ideas and take unfamiliar actions, another challenge arises. You can be a transformed woman or man and get thrown off balance fast enough to make your head spin when you are:

- Exhausted
- Sick
- Hungry
- Overwhelmed
- Offended
- Hormonal
- Stressed

Old patterns become the default behavior when you are anything less than in an optimal state.

Or in other words, at least half the time, you are potentially subjected to a physical or emotional influence that alters your perception of any situation. Nelson Mandela once stated, "Where you stand depends on where you sit."

What is a human being to do? Persevere.

Like yoga or meditation, life is a practice, not a perfect. Eventually, you'll better understand what your body is telling you and determine what is driving your thoughts, words, and actions.

My barometer to understand fear when it appears in my body is simple as it doesn't show up often. When faced with an opportunity that scares me, I jump on it quickly because the knot in my stomach is an indicator that something extraordinary is in the midst. Usually, it's something that invites me to stretch so far beyond what I am currently able to comprehend; I get concerned about whether or not I can handle it.

Contemplating significant opportunities for me is about my physicality but also about the emotional, intellectual, and spiritual investment required. Knowing I'm about to get catapulted into another realm of being transparent and serving others is enticing but scary. Frankly, in spite of all the work I've done, there's still a little voice that questions if I'm good enough.

Fortunately, the fear doesn't hold me long - seconds, minutes perhaps but rarely hours. In the past, it used to be days, weeks, months, years even.

You may have no desire whatsoever to explore the depths of who you are, why you think and react the way you do, and that's ok - no judgment here. One has to be willing and ready to subject the psyche to the ups and downs of their humanity and how their life shapes them.

If nothing else, I trust from this chapter you've considered the epidemic every culture has around making assumptions and from where misunderstandings source. No matter how intelligent you are, emotionally or intellectually, you never know what another person is thinking or why they have that perspective. Never.

Optional Mantras

Everyone is going through something at this moment, I am compassionate rather than judgmental.

I silently project love to those who are the most critical, all they need is someone who believes in them.

It is never my job to judge another person.

"Look at the word responsibility – "response-ability"- the ability to choose your response. Highly proactive people recognize that responsibility. They do not blame circumstances, conditions, or conditioning for their behavior. Their behavior is a product of their own conscious choice, based on values, rather than a product of their conditions, based on feeling ."

- *Stephen Covey*

Chapter 5

Taking Responsibility

Once you take responsibility, where do you bring it? The irony of this chapter is painfully amusing.

Just yesterday I had a conversation with a woman on the WAFW Leadership Team in Bangladesh about some miscommunication and created a space for her to see a different outcome. Today I got a message from her everything got worked out. When I asked the most important things she learned about the process she said, “All the different ways there are to communicate.”

When egos get bruised, feelings get hurt, and one’s efforts don't seem appreciated, anything can happen. It’s tempting to adopt, “an eye for an eye” and throw back at your challenger, the best response to save face or defend your honor. Such fragile beings we are under the thick skin we often show the world.

The irony of where I now sit is because I’m taking something personally when it’s not deliberately intended, I’m choosing to take it that way. Due to my involvement and the depth of relationship I’ve been blessed to build, I feel like a mother defending her children from an injustice. In such moments, I’m not above growling, showing my teeth, or writing what can get perceived in hindsight as a snarky email. If I read my composition, I’d take it as such.

The challenge of any person of integrity is noticing where their practice doesn't align with their teaching. For me also included is calling myself out to bring the situation into a teaching moment. The realization of how sensitive my ego still is when anything I've put blood, sweat, and tears into appears threatened - is a gift. Imagine my eyebrows furrowed, pouting lips, and an overall a disapproving demeanor.

Now that I've taken responsibility for how I feel, what am I going to do with it? The question of the day. As I see it my options are:

- Get on the phone with the person who I feel the most misunderstood by.
- Get creative and explore another solution.
- Withdraw like a child.
- A phone call is forthcoming next week and involves others who aren't available now. Do I have the same conversation twice? Maybe three times? Grrr. Now faced with the question I asked you in the

first paragraph, I've taken responsibility for how I feel, what do I do with it?

Leaving an issue unresolved is an invitation for the imagination to run wild with assumptions and create undesired outcomes.

I feel the energy of a petulant child surfacing, perhaps a temper tantrum brewing fueled by any other time I didn't get my way. Frankly, it's surprising how prevalent this energy is at the moment.

It's one thing to bring the topic of getting offended in class when not amid a situation, then another entirely as I write about it while the emotions are brewing within.

Like a hungry dog holding onto a piece of meat, I snarl at the idea of food getting taken away. Yep, that's a visual representation for you.

It didn't take long to realize what I was feeling. It never takes long for me to take responsibility for more than I need to. Some time ago when the blame stopped and the leader emerged, owning what went wrong in any given situation that I was remotely attached to became second nature.

Acknowledging what could have got said or done differently puts others at ease in an almost magical way. Taking responsibility for one's thoughts and reactions immediately (in most cases) puts the other person at ease.

Looking foolish stopped bothering me decades ago, so that's not what's eating at me. I'm not hormonal at the moment. There is Mercury Retrograde for those of you tuned in to astrology.

So why won't I let go? Twenty years ago I would've written, "Why can't I let go?" It's not that I cannot, of course, I can. I don't want to at the moment. Let's go back to the mother defending her child.

You don't have to look far to find people who get offended easily then get sanctimonious defending what they trust is correct. There are increasingly positive examples available when you want to change gears quickly. However, you'll immediately find people to toss gasoline on your Inferno and others willing to fan the flames to ensure the fire doesn't go out. How helpful. N.O.T.

Regardless of how far you've come on your transformation journey, there will always be another trigger you don't see coming. How can you take what the universe unveils to you and turn the moment into a healing experience?

It's tempting to pile everything else going wrong in your life onto this ONE situation. From the loss of income to health challenges to missed opportunities, the ego can quickly turn a relatively simple misunderstanding into a monumental problem. Does it now make more sense why bored people wreak so much havoc?

You can also go to the other end of the activity spectrum and get busy. The best way to avoid awkward conversations or confrontation is taking on or doing unnecessary work. A distracted mind is a content mind in most cases.

When taking responsibility for your thoughts or actions, I ask you to make every effort to avoid the most common mental trap of using words to describe the situation as:

- Better or worse
- Good or bad
- Right or wrong

Instead, look at how you could've done something differently. Self-judgment is an epidemic already. As uncomfortable as reflection is, hindsight is one of the most significant teaching tools. In my construction industry days, I had a "NEVER AGAIN LIST!" Funny how I cannot recall anything on the list now, but when I made a mistake that cost my boss money it was essential to document the lesson as not to repeat it. In the process of learning it's critical to realize one mistake does not render your judgment forever questionable.

Some of the most significant AH HAs I've seen occur when a woman realizes how she could've thought about something differently.

One homework assignment I gave in Bangladesh requested women to list three triggers or things that bothered them enough to bring sadness. Things that time and time again were problematic emotional issues.

The most common triggers were disrespect and judgment. The next phase of the exercise was to examine how these triggers made these women stronger leaders. A woman's experience induces empathy when she stops getting defensive.

Can you imagine what a game-changing afternoon it was to witness women seeing a different perspective on a behavior or thought process? To most people, the thought of observing actions or reactions as a tool for growth never enters their mind.

Now their hypersensitivity to another's words or actions made sense to them and shed light on a leadership skill that makes them unique.

If I had to break down the process of learning to take responsibility, I'd ask you to look at three phases.

The first component is **becoming aware**, simply noticing where or how you did something that you preferred a different outcome. Admitting the contribution without being too tough on self is a skill that takes practice to build.

The second phase is **stating out loud** to another person when you're sure you've done something. The admission of responsibility builds trust in those to whom you chose to be accountable.

The advanced phase of accountability is true leadership; when others could easily get blamed for something going wrong, and **you take responsibility** for not knowing, guessing, or predicting a situation. It takes a confident person to step into this last phase because there's no room for the ego there.

An example can look like:

- You ask for information and don't get it. It's easier to blame the other person for not giving you what you asked for instead of realizing you could've done a better job following up.
- Assuming someone understands you when there are gaps in your requests. Paraphrasing is a fantastic tool to ensure another person comprehends what you're asking.
- Blaming a busy person for not conveying a vital piece of information that to you seems obvious, instead of asking something like, "What am I not thinking about here that could influence my desired outcome?"

It's far easier to blame someone else than to acknowledge where you could've done something differently. We've all been wrong throughout our life and don't enjoy getting reminded. Insecurities of the past remain hidden when left unaddressed. One can run, but cannot hide.

After a delightful conversation with my husband that began with, "What am I not seeing?" he reminded me of something I hadn't taken note of before. Although my ego can get in the way at times, when I feel I am asked to do anything that occurs to me is WRONG, look out! I will fight for what I trust is right and defend with every ounce of my being what appears to me is accurate or unjust. Regardless.

The key here is to understand people trust what they know, regardless of if it appears as "right" or "wrong" to anyone else. The world is as any one individual sees it. People will fight for what occurs to them is true. A lifetime of conditioning needs time to transform into a different perspective.

Furthermore, the people you surround yourself with either support your increased awareness or reinforce from what you want to move beyond. Select who you share your insights and transformation with carefully.

As you begin to take responsibility for yourself and others, your appreciation for leadership will expand, as will your skill to lead by example. When it's a challenge to maintain consistency, examine the interruptions, recommit to integrity, and choose to turn your observation into a teaching moment.

Helping others feel safe enough to explore who they are, and test skills as they get built is the greatest gift you can give your team, your community, or your family.

By setting an example, you inspire others to take risks and trust what they are capable of accomplishing. The growth you experience will change the way you see the world. Be prepared, you will inspire some and upset others.

When contemplating anything complicated, it helps to look at the overall highest possible outcome as it serves everyone, not just you. Small seemingly insignificant actions can produce extraordinary results in the people who trust you. Welcome to the next phase of leadership.

Optional Mantras

Taking responsibility is only as painful as I make it, I don't know the opinion of the person I am about to speak to, I cannot presume to know their heart.

My thoughts, words, actions, and intentions are powerful, I use them wisely.

"The privilege of a lifetime is to become who you truly are."

- C.G. Jung

Chapter 6

Fake It Till You Make It

When I asked women in Bangladesh if they heard the phrase used to title this chapter, one third raised their hand. Perhaps mostly used in America to put on the face of success when one hasn't fully arrived yet, faking anything is deceitful to the process of transformation.

Inviting a woman to be strong is one thing but asking her to be something she isn't, is another story. Recognizing where fear or apprehension lives in one's self is a necessary component of getting beyond the paralyzing effects of insecurity.

Without offering opportunities for a woman to build on the skills she has, you are asking her to enter the Tour De France without letting her remove the training wheels from her first bicycle.

Authenticity has never been more important than at this moment! If you have a mission and want to create longstanding change, you'll want to give people in the room the opportunity to grow into your invitation.

Allowing a woman or man to gradually move through what she or he has been struggling with for perhaps decades is honoring the process of discovery in a person.

In Bangladesh, there was a woman who took three months to start speaking up in class, and by the end of the fourth month she was standing in the front of the room and heard in the back row. Her process was on her timeline. Was she nudged? Absolutely, but never forced.

There were other women so hungry for the opportunity to speak; you couldn't get a word in until they took a break to breathe.

There were dozens of moments in class where vulnerability ruled the day. If a story from my past of failure or ego getting in the way would reinforce a point, I used it. Women need to know the mentors who show up in their lives are not perfect unless referred to as "perfectly human."

The combination of hundreds or thousands of seemingly unimportant acts, words, and tiny moments are what helps any person feel safe in your presence.

One such act is doing nothing. Seems simple but is likely the most challenging thing for you to do. When considering “nothing” from a different perspective, you’ll soon see how in fact, it is indeed, quite something.

Examples of doing nothing are:

- Listening intently without expressing an opinion or revealing judgment through facial expression.
- Opening your heart to put yourself in another person's shoes.
- Envisioning another with a golden white light surrounding them.
- Praying for another person’s highest good.

When approached by someone who needs help, it’s tempting to solve their problem without knowing that’s what they want. So the next time you’re asked the classic comment, “Have you got a minute?" ask if the person wants you to listen only or offer assistance.

For years I interrupted people mid-speech because I couldn't control the urge to share my comments. Partly due to the nature of my work; healing and nurturing but also because of a vow made decades ago not to watch others suffer.

If I learned anything about suffering it's this:

What I view as suffering may not be another person's version.

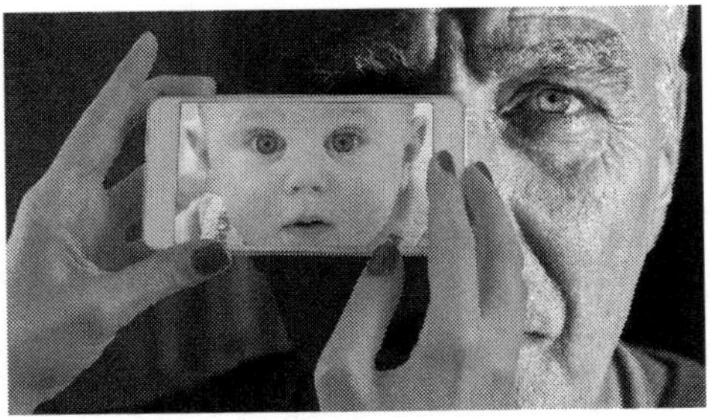

Like women who find their voice and are compelled to use it at every opportunity (some are oblivious to their audiences tolerance to listen), it's easy to impart what's unwelcome with the intention of assisting. I used to get so excited at the opportunity to share what I knew

Early in my leadership journey I often overlooked whether or not my advice was wanted.

Sometimes people will humor you and listen, perhaps fidgeting after a while. Others will start looking at their phone or express through body language when they've had enough.

When you can observe the beauty of such authenticity during this process instead of forming a judgment, you can see the growth. The tricky part is how patient you're willing to be through another person's exploration of self and your ability to communicate before you get frustrated.

In the act of supporting someone, if you get annoyed because you cannot set boundaries, you are faking it as well. Imagine the facial expressions and body language you exhibit once you've had enough of anything. Suddenly helping becomes harmful. The next time a person seeks you out you may choose to be less available; avoiding texts, calls, and messages. You may commit to an appointment, then cancel. The other person can feel neglected, or worse, abandoned.

At times when you have nothing to give, a simple message stating you don't feel well or at your best is perfectly acceptable. Sometimes you must put yourself first and not feel guilty.

Faking how you feel serves no one. Pretending is no way to live a life. Learning how to communicate where you are "emotionally" takes practice. Those who aren't used to your expression of such matters may resist initially, that's their prerogative, and I'd encourage you not to judge them for it. Just as it takes you time to articulate, listening is also a practice.

How can you help someone feel safe enough to be authentic? Find the courage to be your unique self. Be silly, be emotional, be a hot mess if necessary - whatever you are in the moment, don't hide it. Trusting another person with the most delicate elements of your psyche builds trust in your relationship.

After you share, thank the person for helping you feel safe enough to express, for not judging you, and whatever other roles they played for you. One must first give before they are trusted enough to receive.

If building trust with others is a skill you want to work on, be deliberate and make a plan. Opening yourself up to everyone can be exhausting if not done with the utmost integrity. What do I mean by this?

Giving for the sole purpose of getting something in return never works out in the long run. If you happen to receive during the process of your generosity, fantastic - please don't shut yourself down from the gratitude of others. Moreover, get clear on why you're taking the journey in the first place.

Be honest. It's been my experience when I build a skill ultimately to be of more of service to others; the unexpected lessons that accompany my endeavors are easier to digest.

Let's look at strategy now. Are you approaching the giving project from the perspective of who you want to serve or the number of people you want to impact?

Look at the other commitments you have and assess the energy it requires to keep them fulfilled. Look at how many hours of free time you have each week, how many hours of sleep and exercise you want. What's left over?

You may already have a full schedule and the thought of finding time for anything deemed non-essential may be the lowest priority. Be realistic with the time you want to invest. Once you think you have an idea of how much time you've got, add another third extra for the unexpected conversations. Maybe you're better than I am at guessing how long things take. If so then forget about adding the extra third, but if you chronically run late, then consider the reality you'll probably want more time

The bottom line here is, if you want others to be genuine, then you must be the first one. Go out on a limb. Risk being vulnerable. Take a chance on feeling freer than you have in decades. Be willing to let go of judgment.

By dropping the mask of confidence when you don't feel it, you'll inspire others to follow.

Everyone wants to feel appreciated for who they are and struggles to find people they can trust enough to behave as such around.

Be the example. Be the first. Open the door and never look back.

Amelia Earhart

"Greatness does not come from trying to achieve the possible."

— Constance Friday

Chapter 7

Widen The Possibilities

In all transparency, over the last 20 years of committed service to others, the one thing I've noticed about my behavior is when I'm feeling vulnerable, my capacity to widen the possibilities to resolve a problem measurably shrinks.

One of the lines of the WAFW oath is, "Widen my vision for what is possible."

How do you measure a possibility? While facilitating a module on SMART goals, the concept of measuring a result was foreign. Gradually the women could see they were each a possibility in their own right, but getting anyone to explain what swings the pendulum from despair to inspiration isn't one clearly defined moment, it's a series of processes.

Just this morning I had NO desire to get out of bed, my body and mind were both limp. The only thing remotely interesting was watching heart-warming films with happy endings. After an hour or so of honoring what I felt, questions began to arise. Was the feeling I had:

- Exhaustion
- Apathy
- Despair
- Worry
- Loneliness
- Illness
- Hunger
- Overwhelm
- Caffeine deprivation

After checking my calendar for confirmation, I measured how many days of rest I've had since returning home three weeks ago. It was three, three days out of twenty-one. Suddenly it made sense. After five months of rising to a challenge that was emotional, mentally, and physically draining, it occurred to me I deserved a little more than three days of rest. Every other emotion listed as a possibility was, in fact, correct but not the catalyst for what I felt.

How do you widen the possibility for your life in such a state? Although the last descriptor on the list was "overwhelm," any of things listed can toss a person back into old behaviors. While new patterns are still formulating, it's no surprise to see how fragile anyone is in the process of a growth journey. Solid as a steel beam in one moment, thin as a soap bubble the next. For the record, everything in life qualifies as a growth process for me.

The women I've watched in China, Nepal, and Bangladesh have the same waffling moments I do. To their credit, the ability of women in Bangladesh to keep going in the face of illness is quite impressive. I've never seen a country with such a large percentage of health challenges for women in their twenties.

From digestive issues to reproductive problems and depression, women are struggling every day. Furthermore, if there is another family member with health issues, they often suffer in silence. For some, widening the vision for what is possible meant speaking up to their family about what troubled them and getting taken seriously.

There were two women in Bangladesh who most impressed me; each had health issues that may have been too much for me to handle. In addition to university classes, WAFW classes, and familial commitments, each of these women took on leadership roles in addition to everything else they managed in their lives. I've never seen such deliberateness; it was inspiring.

One of these women came to me after a class so distraught because there was no end in sight and she was at her wit's end. After a lengthy discussion, I challenged her to make a video statement I'd record that she could later watch to feel empowered in her low moments. After five or six attempts, we captured the energy, not just the words, of a woman who was courageous enough to take a stand for her health. Watching her declare what she wanted with her hands on her hips was such a thing of beauty.

Often women need help widening their vision. Sitting in a classroom listening to a lecture or participating in an interactive class begins the process, but support is required to continue.

The type of support I'm referring to is tangible. It's women getting together to hold one another when the world feels as though it's imploding.

It's the depth of a gaze that requires no words to convey a belief. Sometimes you need other people to help you see what you're not capable of seeing alone.

I'd be remiss excluding one woman in China who had a similar potential debilitating disease but found the strength to take her university classes, WAFW classes, and perform a leadership role. The only reason I knew about her ailment was from an exercise in class when I asked everyone to share something about themselves; the group would never guess.

The World Academy for the Future of Women invites its members to see the leader inside, draw on her and realize she is capable of changing circumstances in villages, schools, and countries. Each woman I've had the privilege of spending time with has taught me something.

As I sit in the beauty and comfort of my home in North America, oppression in my country seems like a luxury compared to what women around the world get subjected to day in and day out.

There's a term, "glass ceiling" you'll hear in professional circles referring to some invisible barrier women cannot cross that is not there for men. I feel the barriers are self-imposed. There are a few things I've done in my life precisely because someone told me I couldn't. Regardless of whether or not I would enjoy the objective, it became a point to prove that I could accomplish anything my mind got set on doing.

Proving a point isn't the best reason to do something, but it's a heck of a way to get you going!

Let's circle back to holding a vision when exhausted, stressed, or ill. In addition to seeing the future you want, there's an energetic component often ignored. What do I mean?

Consider music for example. Deep notes can feel daunting or heavy - consider this a lower vibration. High notes are light, perhaps envision a fairy flittering about playfully.

Loftier notes carry a higher resonance and allow more flexibility of movement making it easier to sustain momentum.

People who bounce back from difficulties at accelerated speeds have learned to come through or out of low vibrations faster. It's not that these folks are superhuman, they have mood swings like anyone, but the difference is when they fall into a dark place, their baseline attitude enables a faster recovery.

When things don't go as planned and you get caught off-guard, learning to approach any problem from a higher vibration behavior (or a more neutral mind) is a subjective process. Some readily do of their own volition or the assistance of others and move quickly through a problem as water flows around a rock.

Other people immediately take challenges personally and put up quite a fight; they get caught in the downward spiral of emotion going from sadness to despair to hopelessness in a fraction of a second. Often referred to moody, unpredictable or unstable, these folks haven't had many examples of how to emerge gracefully from a challenge by finding the lesson.

At one time I lived in a downward spiral, and I couldn't see any other way out. My default emotion when things went wrong was unworthiness. Once the feeling got a hold of me, I wouldn't let it go. I knew the feeling all too well; I lived in unworthiness for almost thirty years. I quickly spotted this in my classes.

So where and how do you begin to change the way you feel? Again, subjective to each of you based on the mind space you occupy at any given moment before the downward spiral begins.

When each "emotional high" is loftier than the last, it gets easier to stay out of the emotional molasses that ego lives to propagate. Ego is not your friend. The same way sugar feeds cancer cells, ego fuels low vibration thoughts and feelings.

Especially during hormonal swings, women experience such a wide range of emotions, discomfort and physical energy. Regardless of your gender, there are a variety of things you can attempt to bring you out of a slump.

Here are some ways to change your state of being:

- Jump up and down.
- Take off your shoes and stand outside in the grass.
- Stand on your head.
- Breathe deeply for 3 minutes.
- Drink a tall glass of water and imagine you are a fluid being.
- Go to the bathroom and imagine the stress leaving your body while you eliminate.
- Pull a hair from your head and imagine with it came the plug holding all your turmoil, then burn the hair in the flame of a candle or flush it down the toilet.
- Play some fast-paced music and dance your tail off.
- Watch an inspiration video on YouTube.
- If you have a drum, rattles or an instrument, play it.
- Get your hands in the soil.
- Burn some incense and imagine your troubles dissipating like the smoke.

Sometimes widening the vision for what is possible begins with changing a mood. From there anything is possible.

Let's imagine you already have a sense of what you'd like to do in the next phase of your life. How much time do you dedicate each day or week to creating this future? Whatever it is, I challenge you to increase it by ten percent. Widening the possibility for your life requires steadfast commitment, a series of consistent small actions, and support from others who can see perhaps a broader future than you are capable of comprehending.

Find one or two people you can count on to lift your state of being when times get tough, value them like gold. Then find someone you can extend the same courtesy to because the more you pay it forward and share what you've learned, the faster the state of all women changes. One woman's victory is every woman's success. Inspiring change globally or in your family begins wherever you start it.

Who will you widen the vision of possibility for today?

"You may have to fight a battle more than once to win it.."

- Margaret Thatcher

Chapter 8

Living An Oath

Every member of the WAFW learns the oath in Module 1 of the academy. As you see each line, imagine what goes through the mind of a college-age woman in a developing country as she reads it for the first time.

As a member of the World Academy for the Future of Women, I am committed to the advancement and acceleration of women's leadership worldwide.

I am inspired through the discovery of my passion, my purpose, and my path to success.

I am courageous and act with honesty and integrity.

I go beyond my personal and geographic boundaries.

I am generous with my time and resources.

I honor and respect the rights and dignity of all people.

I widen my vision for what is possible and strengthen my capacity to lead.

I live a meaningful and fully expressed life.

As a global citizen, I take responsibility for my actions and live my life in harmony with the planet.

I make this oath freely and give my word to keep it.

Now imagine a woman in a developing country reading the oath and getting asked to live by it, much different than reciting. The one thing that most attracted me to WAFW was the oath and the fact that I already lived by it without having read it.

In China, Nepal, and Bangladesh every academy member, in the beginning, struggled with the concept of becoming a leader. In part from the examples set by their respective governments. Even if a woman held a political office, she did not always yield the power one would expect.

Like many people, young women struggle to see themselves as a person who attracts followers. By the definition of some, if no one looks to you for direction, you aren't leading anyone anywhere.

However, if you consider leadership as a concept that begins within an individual rather than a discipline requiring people to control – you'll start to understand the complexity of what WAFW asks of its members.

Over one thousand women and some men age seventeen to twenty-six have taken this oath over the last ten years. Each academy member approaches the declaration from the lens by which they've been conditioned to see the world.

In China, there are public spaces where parents can post a photo of their daughter as an eligible bride. I have yet to see one for myself but have heard stories from many about their existence.

Unlike the United States, women in all three countries where WAFW facilitates leadership, experience extreme pressure to marry.

A family considers it an embarrassment when a young woman hasn't wed by the age of twenty-five.

Women get told their eggs will dry up, they won't be able to conceive children, and that no one will want them. Mother's, grandmother's, aunties and cousins all join the mission to find a husband for a woman of marrying age.

I imagine a commitment to the advancement and acceleration of women's leadership worldwide sounds excellent in the beginning, but when it comes down to it, many resign to family pressure or find the commitment too challenging to manage.

As the Start-Up Coordinator in both Nepal and Bangladesh, I saw women excited in the beginning but dropping out during the first module. The academy requires attendance in five mandatory classes per week averaging eight to ten hours of a members time.

What most women misunderstand is the level of commitment required to become a leader. The beginning is the toughest because we ask women to look at themselves and to take responsibility for how they think, speak and act. Facilitators make every effort to set an ideal example for the members.

Let's go back to the first line of the oath, "committed to the advancement and acceleration of women's leadership worldwide." It's one thing to say it and another to live it. The intention behind this statement is that every woman in the academy ultimately starts or participates in a project that supports one of the seventeen United Nations Sustainability Goals (SDGs). The projects reinforce the commitment we ask members to make and bring women closer to the concept of worldwide.

Once alumni of WAFW, members can assist the startup of an academy in another country - further deepening the meaning of line one of the oath. Grace came to Bangladesh from China to be of assistance. She took time off work and paid her way to advance and accelerate women's leadership worldwide.

Line two: I am inspired through the discovery of my passion, my purpose, and my path to success. The concept of knowing one's "passion or purpose" is confounding to some in the beginning. Did you know what you were passionate about as a college student? I didn't realize my calling until I was thirty-five.

Without knowing the path one is destined to take, empowerment through a path to success seems more comfortable to believe. Founder of WAFW, Jerrie Ueberle will tell you her curriculum is a path to success, but she's not alone.

In China, corporate supervisors have stated that women who come from WAFW are stronger leaders than some men in their fifties! You ought to see the eyes enlarge when this fact gets shared during the recruitment process.

Line three: I am courageous and act with honesty and integrity. How many people in your life live by this statement? In a world where it's easier to blame another then take responsibility, this line of the oath is one of the most challenging. To be honest with self requires a tremendous amount of courage.

Whether a woman recognizes the justification used to make excuses for her thoughts or actions or the codependent behavior she encourage in others, living a life of integrity starts the moment she stops lying to herself.

Gradually, a woman learns how to articulate her realizations and improves her communications skills along the way. If a member family isn't initially a safe place to share what she feels, we encourage her to share the lessons of the academy in a way that promotes curiosity. Many a member have reported an improvement in the way they converse at home. Some have begun talking for the first time while others reignite dialogue that some were resigned to being long gone.

Line four: I go beyond my personal and geographic boundaries. For most women, this declaration represented speaking up because silence provided safety or essentially, invisibility.

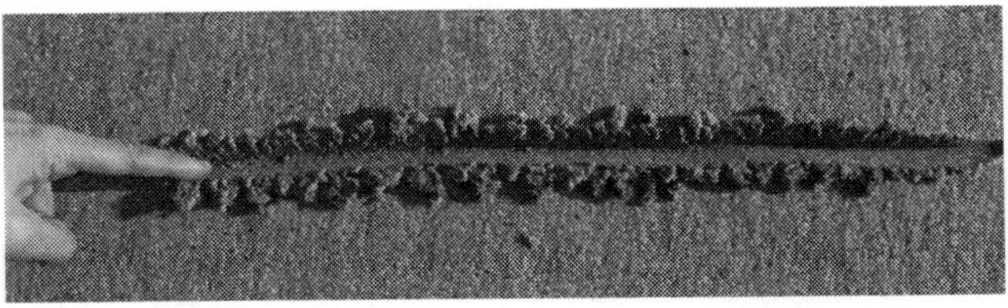

Most Americans when hearing the term "geographic" boundary think of leaving their state, country, or continent. For some women in my classes, crossing that line of safety meant getting up from their chair to speak. Everyone defines what captivates them differently.

Line five: I am generous with my time and resources. Generosity, when you don't have much, makes this concept perplexing to most of the women. Their most valuable commodity is time. One of the requirements of the academy is a filling out a weekly time analysis sheet to plan for the future you want to create.

Like almost every member, I didn't enjoy this exercise. The sheet felt constricting, controlling and burdensome. I didn't realize the value at the time but gradually came to appreciate it as a mapping tool.

You'd be surprised how busy some of the women in Bangladesh were. Looking at their sheets, almost every one hour block of time between 6 am, and 11 pm got filled in, leaving no time for spontaneity. Although I never saw the sheets in China, I recall those academy women just as busy, and they lived on campus.

The most significant lesson brought into class about the generosity of ones time was;

"Don't be afraid to put a limit on how much time you're willing to give someone. Respect yourself and honor your time; no one else will do it for you."

Line six: I honor and respect the rights and dignity of all people. Surprisingly, women rarely will women apply this concept to themselves before others.

In developing countries where gender equality is far from achieved, self-respect isn't an openly discussed topic. When women are shaped by a culture to accept certain practices and tolerate being a second class citizen, this concept must begin with the members themselves before women applying it to others. Some fight it. Many mothers disagree.

Some parents believe they are protecting their

children when they purposefully avoid bringing attention to misconduct. In cultures where women get blamed for rape, not many families want to risk the scrutiny and instead focus on the shame. Countless victims get left in the wake of unbearable judgment.

In one of the earliest coaching circles when women felt safe enough to talk about some of these assaults they experienced, the energetic shift in the room resulting from a collective sigh of relief was tangible. That afternoon coaching circle was the catalyst for this book. Women realized they weren't alone.

Line 7: I widen my vision for what is possible and strengthen my capacity to lead. There's nothing like watching a woman light up when you see her step into the possibility for her life.

It's been a privilege over the last twenty years to hold space for thousands of women of all ages to see how their life can be. Seeing, believing, and trusting the possibility are three completely different things. Perhaps a play on language, to me belief will never be as strong as trusting. To "trust" is absolute, it's a certainty that regardless of where the path takes you, all roads ultimately lead you through the necessary phases of development, so you're ready for what's next.

Sometimes a woman must first lead herself through trying times so when she leads others; there is more confidence in her capacity to hold space for others. It's not a leaders responsibility to help others solve their problems, but more to help people see alternatives and realize solutions they hadn't been able to see alone. Genuine leadership is empowering others to find answers.

Line 8: I live a meaningful and fully expressed life. Another multi-faceted interpretation, the living of a fully expressed life means something unique to every person who takes the time and fully digests the concept.

My present definition is: sharing what I know with the freedom to travel and change lives globally. What's yours?

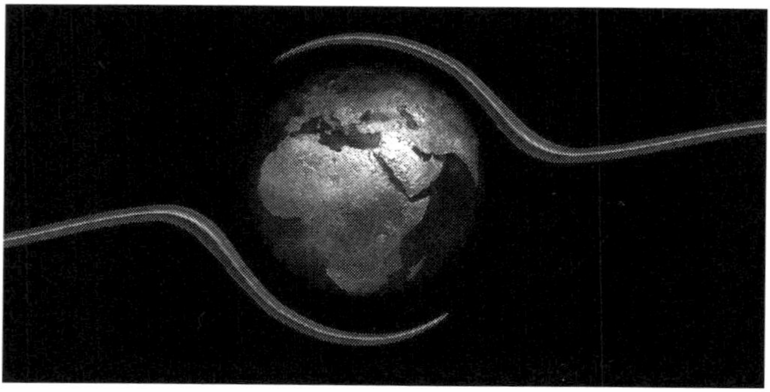

Verbal expression isn't the only way to live fully. One of the most exquisite things I saw in Bangladesh was women who traditionally wore black hijab's beginning to wear color! The light they brought into a room could make anyone with a heart smile.

There is one woman who comes to mind that took three months to begin speaking up in class. In the beginning, she whispered. After sixteen weeks she was standing up in the front of the classroom, and you could hear her from the back of the room.

Through a woman's life the definition of what living fully expressed, changes. The realization of a woman's talent gets more comfortable for her after she accomplishes her first goal. As more opportunities come and more successes follow, she redefines the expression of what it means to live fully.

Line 9: As a global citizen, I take responsibility for my actions and live my life in harmony with the planet. In the beginning, women struggle taking responsibility for their actions. Historically, most people witness or experience blame for the way another person feels or acts. It's a classic exchange in families or close relationships to hear, "You made me..." when a person hasn't learned how to be accountable for their actions.

So many women feel they have no choice in circumstances of pressure. It's not that there isn't a choice; it was the consequences of what they choose that's uncomfortable and in many cases too scary. It's not just women; not many people have the skill to navigate uncertainty. The fear of the unknown cripples most of humanity.

The funny thing is, most times the fear people create in their mind is far worse than what happens when they find the courage to take action.

It's easy to look at any successful person and believe they have always been confident; nothing could be farther from the truth. Success is the culmination of thousands of often small, invisible choices and actions a person takes for decades before they "arrive."

The transformation members of the academy experience are significant when they choose to live this oath. It'd be wonderful if we could get them to open up on camera before they begin the program and share their challenges, but I understand why they don't. It's hard enough to admit to one's self the traits one isn't happy with, never mind share them with another person you barely know.

Seeing the women of the WAFW, especially the women who step up to leadership roles, blossom and find the leader within pales any success of my own.

If the oath resonates with you, WAFW is always looking for facilitators. Go to www.wafw.org for more information.

Optional Mantras

Before I lead others, I must first lead myself.

I am capable of being the leader I never had.

It is my responsibility to inspire those around me to be the best people they can be.

"Keep your thoughts positive because your thoughts become your words. Keep your words positive because your words become your behavior. Keep your behavior positive because your behavior becomes your habits. Keep your habits positive because your habits become your values. Keep your values positive because your values become your destiny."

- *Mahatma Gandhi*

Chapter 9

Operating Principles

In addition to the Oath, WAFW has a set of Requirements and Operating Principles our members are expected to follow. For this chapter, I'll focus on the influence of the

Principles as they relate to a woman's transition from oppression to trusting herself.

I've yet to meet a woman who at some point in life felt she didn't have a choice about at least one uncomfortable decision she had to make. How do you get a woman to trust that she DOES have a voice and a choice?

For starters, you provide an environment safe enough to let her practice using her voice. You give her opportunities to make choices, to take responsibility for her thoughts, language, and her actions. Then you encourage her to extract the lesson from what appears to go completely off plan.

Part of WAFW best practices is to encourage a transition of language. Taking simple terms and replacing them with one word can significantly change the outcome of a situation. For example:

- Right and wrong
- Good and bad
- Better and worse

When you transform a statement into a question and interchange the word "different" in place of the other words ingrained into our language since birth, something remarkable happens; a distinct expansion of thought and development of other possibilities occurs.

Let's look at a common miscommunication. For example, a woman new to leadership requesting something from her team and the request gets percieved as a demand. The team member is offended, retaliates, and an emotional exchange ensues. Bruised egos fuel hurtful comebacks until an impasse halts progress.

Instead of blaming the leader for being bossy or insensitive (clearly, she's sensitive since her teammate's response triggered her) what if the leader chose her words, differently?

What if the leader made her initial request using different words, formulating what sounded like a request instead of a demand? A sensitive situation may have gotten avoided.

Last week I was on the phone with a leader who experienced this situation. Early in the conversation, the leader was compelled to defend her actions instead of considering what she could've done differently. The circumstances didn't matter; I could've let her spend an hour complaining about the details of the situation, but that wouldn't have been the best use of our time.

Eventually, the leader realized she did have other options. I'm happy to report she met with the woman who misunderstood her, took responsibility for how she said what she did and apologized. As a result, both women are now working well together again, and have learned a valuable lesson about making communication assumptions.

Had the leader not reached out to me in despair, she may never have learned the value of three more operating principles,

“Think about how you think,” “Nothing changes if nothing changes,” and “Point of view.”

It took repeatedly asking the leader, “How could you have asked the team member to take action differently?” before it became clear that there are a variety of ways people prefer to get communicated with, no two individuals are alike. This realization was the biggest takeaway the leader had from this challenge.

Once upon a time, “better” was a commonly used word in my vocabulary. Everything I did was an exercise in constant improvement. Maybe I had a point to prove, but every project I took on had to bigger, better, or more significant the last. Now I merely ask from a non-judgmental perspective, how I can do things differently. The rest of the world outside WAFW can stick with the labels of good or bad, better or worse, right or wrong; it's not my mission to transform everyone outside of WAFW. All I can do is set an example with my actions.

Of all the requirements I attempt to infuse into members, the one I struggle with the most myself is, "Reasons don't equal results." Every time I find myself explaining why I didn't accomplish anything I said I'd do, I hear an excuse. My words sound like a justification to ease the shame or embarrassment for lack of following through. How can I facilitate one thing and not practice it? Sometimes I still wrestle with the difference between a reason and an excuse. How do you differentiate the two?

Over the last two years, the next principle I'll share has been the easiest, "Choose something bigger than yourself." I've taken a lot of flack from some family members about this one. What began almost five years ago as a choice to walk away from gainful employment to realize a dream, has been anything but smooth.

The only reason family is mentioned and not acquaintances is because I've let go of many relationships that didn't support the risks I chose to take. Although some don't outright say they think I'm nuts, I suspect they believe it. My stepmother and my son are the only two people who have been bold enough to question my intention. Happy to report, my son understands how fulfilled I get from serving WAFW, and he's now "happy that I'm happy."

After reclaiming my voice some twenty years ago and making a commitment to support other women, I've never looked back. I could no longer watch women suffering from the sidelines. Metaphorically losing your voice or choosing silence to appease others feels like one of the worst injustices aside from physical and sexual abuse. Women deserve to get heard.

Life appears far less complicated when you play the game according to other people's rules. It's easier to avoid conflict when remaining compliant. But compliance is dull and lacks imagination. There will always be some who secretly work toward creating a different world, but it takes longer to attract followers when you're worried about getting found out.

One principle that can easily interchange with a line in the oath, "Live life fully expressed," is bold and daring. First, you need to figure out what it means for you. A full expression of your life can be verbal, as in voicing your opinion in casual conversation, public speaking, singing, or acting.

Another way to express can be through movement or art. Dance, athletics, writing, music, architecture or cooking all qualify as a means of sharing your passion. Consider what brings you the most joy and find a way to incorporate it daily. Writing and speaking are two things that feed me while serving others.

Part of the mission of every facilitator for WAFW is to help members realize they are a possibility. One of the reasons for the success of this ten-year program is the variety of exposure women get from people all over the world. Many volunteers come from America, but also from Australia, the Netherlands, Venezuela, and China. Each facilitator leaves the comfort of their own country, their families and jobs or businesses to share a unique perspective on the curriculum. For five weeks facilitators experience a new culture and are immersed in university life and often the lives of the members. By setting an example of generosity and courage, women learn how diverse one can live a life.

So many entrepreneurs began their journeys because they weren't employable or couldn't hold down a job. What does living life "fully expressed" mean to you?

Once you figure out what a full expression of your life looks like, find people to support you in living that way. Academy members have a built-in support network and learn how to receive just as much as they learn to give. Without support, it's a lonely journey, not impossible but also not as insightful.

Mentorship plays a critical component of any transformational path. There are times you cannot see the forest through the trees so to speak. What is evident to others can remain oblivious to you until someone points it out. It's also nice to have someone bear witness to your face palm moments. Not only do you feel a sense of accomplishment, but your mentor also takes pride in what you've realized. As Stephen Covey would say, "A win-win!"

Aside from everything else you've read about the WAFW, what I haven't shared about the exchange between facilitators and members is another fantastic principle I live by: "Be inspired, be grateful, be generous."

Getting inspired by academy members is effortless. You can't help but get moved by the stories of what women overcome. Then in addition to their stories, you have the privilege of seeing how they grow through adopting all the academy has to offer.

Creating a space for women to feel safe requires skill. Once you see the first shift in awareness of a woman stepping into leadership, you more fully understand the responsibility and know it's a privilege to receive their trust.

Gratitude is a concept an entire book could easily get dedicated to, but for now, I invite you to imagine the power of being grateful for every experience life has presented you. Can you allow your imagination to find an uplifting moment amid an otherwise tragic event? You might call the development of such an understanding as, "Gratitude 2.0" because not everyone can adopt this advanced way of thinking.

The most challenging emotional or intellectual moments regardless of what country I've been in have provided the most significant realizations. Even with my fair share of physical challenges, a new perspective revealed itself like a reward for a job well done. Reinforcement of your choices are found anywhere you dare to look.

Although the words make sense, adopting the principle of having all the time in the world, takes deliberate effort. My body and spirit agree, but once the ego gets going, the mind struggles. Fortunately, this dilemma doesn't happen often, but when it does focusing on the possibility that lies ahead is frustrating.

Time is a multi-faceted concept. The relationship most women have with time is that of scarcity – there's never enough! If you ask the women in Bangladesh about time, you'd be surprised how many of them manage to attend WAFW classes with everything else they have going on. Some have up to two-hour commutes in each direction to university, then their course load, and family obligations. It's no wonder, so many of them are exhausted.

Women in America share the same challenges:

- Not enough time to sleep.
- Exercise?!
- Practice self-care.
- Have fun (what's that?).

Circling back around to the timesheet WAFW asks members to do weekly, we have the same amount of time every other person on the planet has. How we choose to spend it defines what is essential.

If you were to die tomorrow, will you have said everything to your loved ones you wanted to? Will you have regrets about all the things you delayed until you could make time? Will you have lived a life that made a difference in the world?

It's only in the last few years that I can honestly say, if my time was up today, I could go in peace. The people I care deeply for know I love them, I've taken more risks than most and had the privilege to share my experiences with those who found them helpful.

What are the operating principles by which you live? Perhaps I cheated by using WAFWs, but they fit. I see the need to *create my own set*, and maybe one day I'll make the time to do so. Perhaps it'll turn into a workshop or a course. If that's of interest to you, let me know by sending an email to leslie@lesliekarenhammond.com and in the subject line write: Personal Operating Principles workshop.

Examples of A Personal Oath

I respect the rights and dignity of all people, starting with me.

I take bold action in service to others.

To serve others in the highest possible capacity, I maintain optimal physical, mental, spiritual and emotional health.

"Life will eventually bring you to your knees. Either you'll be on your knees cursing the universe and begging for a different life, or you'll be brought to your knees in gratitude and awe, deeply embracing the life you have, too overwhelmed by the beauty of it all to stand or even speak. Either way they're the same knees."

—*Jeff Foster*

Chapter 10

What It's Like Facilitating

First and foremost, volunteering for WAFW changes you. If you are a heart-centered person, your eyes will open to the commonalities of the human condition globally. The way you see the world and your part in it also shifts.

What surprised me the most was how warmly received I was into countries I'd never visited. Granted, when a university and the WAFW know you're coming, preparations are made. For those about to take the first facilitation assignment, there is a delightful sense of getting treated like royalty. Perhaps somewhat stated from an egoistic perspective, who wouldn't enjoy seeing a sign with their name on it when arriving at an airport in a foreign country? For me, it never gets old.

To have people who have only heard about you be so gracious and welcoming is beautiful. I've always felt extremely cared for and safe.

I'd love to know what secret expectations the people who pick up facilitators have. In China, the Ambassador Leader is a coveted role because they go to the airport to receive incoming facilitators as well as drop them off at departure.

The first time in China was unique in so many ways. My first time in Asia for starters. Conducting leadership training wasn't new but doing so for college-age women was. Fortunately, the English capacity of most members we encountered was strong enough to feel understood. Sometimes one has to ask questions differently when body language conveys confusion, but communication was never an issue.

In our China classes, all the PowerPoint's got translated. Often we had a translator too. Usually, an academy member volunteered because they knew it was a terrific opportunity to improve their English. For some facilitators, navigating the translation process while presenting takes time to adjust to because the translator takes almost 50% of your class. Remembering to stop at the end of every sentence or two got more comfortable, but some struggled. When one is passionate, they want to keep the momentum of topic going and get so excited they forget to pause.

The time zone difference of twelve hours took a few days to adjust to fully. It's not uncommon to arrive around midnight, then after the hour or so drive to campus, and a compulsion to unpack upon arrival, my head usually hit the pillow around 4 am.

Bringing some food with me (smoothie mix, wheatgrass, and supplements) made it possible to skip breakfast which got served from 6 am to 7 am.

The increased enthusiasm one feels they can last for one to three days before your body reminds you-you're not superhuman and you need to get to bed early for a few nights to assist in fully acclimating to another time zone. The time it takes is different for everyone.

There are a lot of people reaching out to you; Ambassadors, Assistants, Translators, other facilitators - each playing a unique role in getting you settled. Your assistant is there for anything you may have forgotten to bring; they can bring you to local shops for toiletries or offer suggestions for things to see when you have time.

Translators are conscientious about understanding your material and usually want to meet with you to review your PPTs.

In the "Handover process," at every module's end the outgoing facilitator shares their experience and offers things like:

- What they covered in their module.
- Who are the rock stars of their classes.
- Who the most challenged members in the class are.
- Tips on technical things they endured.
- What surprised them the most.
- An introduction in at least two seminars to meet members.
- The routine they found most helpful.
- Must see things or food they enjoyed.

Part of my handover process included taking facilitators off campus on a quick bus ride to the "Waka," more of a nickname for a department store that carried items ranging from food to clothing and almost everything in between.

The one thing that surprised most facilitators:

no amount of training can prepare you for the emotional investment you make in the members. Some grow on you in ways you could never imagine and become part of the very fabric of your being.

Women who are ready trust you such at an accelerated rate, some are willing to open up about their lives and challenges seeking a compassionate ear or sometimes advice. The Western perspective is entirely different than most Eastern practices. Therefore what facilitators offer sounds good in theory but often takes a while to implement. There will always be exceptions to the rule, consider how long it takes you to adopt a new practice.

Another thing that made the first trip to China so special was arriving during the National Holiday. Within three days I was off to visit three different villages over four days. Four hours of taxi's, bus and a train ride later we got picked up and transported to a farming community. It was the first week of October, and the streets lined with corn drying along much of the rural route; whole cobs piled sometimes covered with a tarp if it just rained and kernels raked out like a sea of yellow. The taxi went from one side of the road to the other weaving in between oncoming traffic and miles of corn.

Two of the places I visited felt like "villages." Narrow dirt roads in some areas, street vendors, farms or factories reinforced the image most imagine a village to be.

The second location I wouldn't call a village. It was more urban and easily could've been in a section of New York City. The homeowners had a business; the apartment was modern, beautiful and shiny.

The acceptance into people's homes and the hospitality shared went beyond anything I ever could've imagined. Children come to visit, many who have never seen a foreigner. There were lots of photos,. Friends of the hosts would come sharing stories and asking questions. In some instances, a master bedroom got offered for the evening's accommodations.

I felt like I was in another home, meeting distant family I didn't know existed. A heck of a start to any foreign travel experience, the following four weeks delivered an equally fantastic immersion into another culture.

Facilitating doesn't always leave time to visit landmarks too far off campus, but you'll see enough to appreciate the country you visit.

The entire experience isn't without its challenges. The more flexible you are, the more you'll adjust to last-minute class schedule or classroom changes, technical difficulties, or food options.

In China, the accommodations were in a foreign faculty building and comfortable. I highly recommend a VPN. There's Wi-Fi, but it has its moments. Without a VPN you can forget about getting into Google, Facebook or most other Western social media platforms. I couldn't access my email without a VPN. The most widely used social media is WeChat. I'd encourage you to begin using it in the states to get your friends, family, or clients accustomed to using it.

The apartments were spacious; the food was western for the most part, there was a sterilized water machine on each floor and laundry facilities. You meet people from across the globe who take teaching assignments and have their families with them. There were more children than I expected. There is a gathering space known as Bridge Cafe on the first floor with lots of seating and another Wifi network. If you crave more diversity in your food, you can eat here at your own expense. They serve meals, coffee, and dessert.

Expect your heart to be captured by the WAFW members and the culture to open your eyes. My only expectation was to fall in love, and it happened. For everything you read in the media about China, to me, they were a people of heart. I never once felt anything but welcomed, valued, and appreciated.

The currency rate is approximately six Yuan to a dollar. Money stretches the farthest in China.

The next country I facilitated in was Nepal. Another location with a relatively high English comprehension, most college staff were easy to communicate with as were 95 percent of the members. Unlike China, we rarely needed a translator.

Sunrises from my bedroom window were a sight to behold in the Kathmandu Valley. The orange ball of fire rising from between the mountain peaks every morning started each day with a smile.

The Nepal WAFW located in a densely populated area produced sounds of a city; ranging from the beeping of scooters, cars, buses, trucks, motorbikes, and bicycles to dogs, roosters, and music.

A culture steeped in Buddhism, you'll find temples on every street, on every corner in some neighborhoods. And festivals! October and the first two weeks of November get reserved for celebrating a variety of gods and goddesses, as well as trips out of the valley back to the village of origin.

One of my favorite things about Nepal is the greeting exchanged, Namaste. Used for hello and goodbye, of the hundreds of people I encountered there were only a few that looked at me oddly and didn't return the greeting. Such a simple expression yet one almost guaranteed to bring smiles to the face of every person making the gesture. On another note of exchange, the currency rate is approximately ten Nepalese rupees to a dollar.

In addition to the beauty of the mountains surrounding the valley, another visual delight is the colorful buildings and the women's clothing. Between the visuals and the spicy food, expect to get stimulated on many levels. A word to the wise, don't bring white clothing. The water often has high mineral content and can discolor items.

The women of Nepal much as women in China have not ventured too far from home. It's customary to live with your parents until you are married. In a country where child brides are still a common village practice, you'll also find the dowry system and concerned parents when a woman hits thirty and remains unwed. Familial pressure kindled by culture is still a reality for most. There were a few women in my classes whose fathers supported their daughters desire to study, work and forge a path of independence.

My second Nepal academy experience was unique from both China and the first trip to Kathmandu; we had men in the academy.

The college had a fair amount of men in the Bachelor of Social Work program, and to attain our goal of one hundred members, we brought men into the academy. These college-age men were learning how to support women in leadership.

One of our class requirements is attendance in weekly coaching sessions. Everyone sits in a circle and asks for help, discusses a challenge with the curriculum, or shares something personal. The men had coaching independent of women. In one of these circles, fifteen men came with open minds and surrounded me with genuine curiosity. I loved the energy of the group once they began to speak up.

One burning question a member had that never occurred to me as a concern was, "What if these women get empowered then abuse it?" Heads around the circle began to nod in agreement. My response – "A woman who feels threatened because she has no support, may behave in such a manner. Women who don't have to fight to hold a position and have men who respect them will not abuse power." The response seemed to appease the fear.

The men of the academy were surprisingly supportive of the women in their lives. One man during an interview expressed his frustration with women who don't believe they can accomplish something. He said, "If women believe they can do anything they want, they'll find a way to do it." Impressive for a man in his early twenties.

Having no biological daughters, falling in love with the Nepalese members was easy, but with the men, I almost felt like I was cheating on my son.

What I found interesting was my relationship with many of the women. Fulfilling as it was, with the exception of my first trip, it was not as emotionally intense as in China or Bangladesh.

I'm a HUGE hugger and didn't get my first deep hug from a member till my last week. It's entirely possible I was so exhausted by the startup mission that I wasn't open to receiving. It doesn't feel likely as hugs charge instead of draining my energy but who's to say?

A few other notable items:

- Expect frequent power outages that don't last long.

- Although not necessary, I still used a VPN.
- Bring additional passport photos.

My Bangladesh experience was much different than China or Nepal and deserves its own chapter.

"The truth is, unless you let go, unless you forgive yourself, unless you forgive the situation, unless you realize that the situation is over, you cannot move forward."

- *Steve Maraboli*

Chapter 11

Bangladesh

Part of my fondness of the Bengali women and the university that hosted us is because I spent a total of three and a half months in Dhaka.

During this time I went through an election,

part of the winter, and the spring. I've never seen such colorfully dressed women. Either in hijabs or saris, I interpreted the festive fabrics as one of the few forms of self-expression a woman can have.

The Bengalese are passionate people. They are the only country in the world to go to war over the threat of losing their mother tongue. They celebrate life with spicy food, prayer, colorful clothing, music, and often loud voices.

Around the election, there were countless rallies (more like parades) in the streets bringing traffic to a standstill. Once I heard what sounded like a marching band at 5:30 am! It wasn't uncommon to also hear a concert begin at 10 or 10:30 pm. Thank goodness for earplugs, and a wall hung air conditioner to drown out the noise.

One of the most valuable lessons I learned about the startup process of bringing a WAFW to a new university, in a culture I'd never experienced was; BE FLEXIBLE. There were multiple schedule changes to accommodate holidays and closures around the election. There were three different campus buildings members came from, one thirty or more minutes away based on traffic.

Traffic was unlike anything I've ever seen! Not to mention, this country is the rickshaw capital of the world. Since I was living in the heart of the Dhaka, I heard the city begin to waken around seven am and settle down for the night at midnight or later.

Unlike Nepal where facilitators stayed on campus, in Dhaka our apartment was a short drive or a fifteen-minute walk. The trip had taken as few as three minutes and as many as ninety during the election. I found the bumper to bumper convergence of bicycles, rickshaws, cycle-driven flatbeds, cars, trucks, scooters, buses, and motorcycles to be fascinating. The cacophony of horns blowing was surreal and constant. Traffic lights are more decoration than useful. And no one thinks anything of making a right turn from the left lane.

The other most valuable thing I took from my time in Bangladesh, was the inspiration for this book. Until now, there hasn't been much mention of my background but to fully comprehend the intensity of what I felt the night this book was birthed, I will share my story as succinctly as possible.

My mother died in a car accident when I was eighteen months old; I was sitting next to her on a journey to relocate our family. After her death, I lived with grandparents for two years until my father remarried. Another relocation brought me to the east coast where I've lived most of my life. My heritage is Native American from a tribe in the Southwest. As a young adult, I visited there a few times but never stayed longer than ten months.

I was always a head-strong child. After a tumultuous relationship with my stepmother, I moved out at age sixteen. Within two years I met my son's father, the closest I imagined a soul mate was in my youth. Our friendship turned into courtship and ultimately a difficult eighteen-year marriage. He was an alcoholic.

After fielding his motorcycle accidents - the first one the most serious (I found out I was pregnant while he was in the Intensive Care Unit after drinking and driving), multiple incarcerations, and the emotional trauma that accompanied these events, I found the beginnings of my purpose.

Going from a fiercely independent young woman to a compliant wife to keep the peace was a necessary part of my evolution. It was through my marriage turmoil I realized my ability to help other women heal from the wounds of their past. I'm a certified Karuna Reiki Master teacher, have studied with

Peruvian shamans in the Amazon rain forest, Machu Picchu, and with North American healers.

My work transitioned in the last few years from following my teachers instruction to following my intuition. My clients have experienced outstanding results. It's in my blood to help those suffering. As an empath, I readily sense the energy of a room, a person, or a place. It's my calling to work primarily with women.

Circling back to the most valuable lesson I learned in Dhaka; sometimes you don't need to do anything but listen and hold the space for others to just "be." Hence the title, Holding Space. I'd never felt as helpless as in the moments of watching and listening to women empty their emotions into a room full of other women they barely knew.

There were countless exercises for women to let go parts of her past that haunted her, and opportunities to share how she's transformed since joining the WAFW. Several times women broke down in tears in front of the class after confessing they got raped or assaulted. Class members rushed from their seats to hold each woman courageous enough to be vulnerable .

The classroom remained emotionally charged in a way no other academy classroom ever was; we called it Magic Room 405. There were no decorations on the walls or brightly colored paint; our class looked from the outside like any other room.

There was no one specific moment women began opening up; most were unknown to one another in spite of attending the same school. Their majors varied from English and Humanities to Business to Computer Science and Journalism. Their ages ranged from eighteen to twenty-five. All were single.

It's been my practice to remain as transparent as possible when facilitating to show the journey of a woman that includes difficulties to inspire the tenacity for rising above one's circumstance. In reflecting my humanity, women permitted themselves to reveal their truth.

In addition to the cultural shaping of a woman in a Muslim country, there is a deep seeded fear many women face - being out too long after dark. Since many crimes committed against women go unpunished, parents and often the university administration, encourage women to get home early. Traveling alone outside the city limits is a rarity for most women.

Additionally, women are conditioned to believe any assault against them is their fault, and it's unsafe for them to travel alone. In the villages, many are oblivious to the opportunities an education can provide. If a family needs to eat and working provides nourishment, an income trumps education.

Hearing first-hand the opinion of some men on where women stand in a culture opened my eyes! When flying from Nepal to Dhaka, the flight was mostly men. The gentlemen in the seats to my left appeared friendly enough when they asked who I was and why I was going to Bangladesh.

I proudly declared I was from the WAFW and headed to University Liberal Arts Bangladesh (ULAB) to facilitate a leadership program intended to promote gender equality, advocate for social justice and empower women. A young man in perhaps his thirties from the row of seats in front of me turned around looked me square in the eyes and said, "Gender equality will never happen."

Then an exchange in Bangla ensued between many of the men in this group across a few rows of seats, twelve to fifteen I'm guessing. I heard a few select words peppered amongst their mother tongue, “American” and “ULAB” to be precise. Then a casual gaze in my direction. At that moment I had to choose between engaging in a debate with no backup or appealing to the men’s sense of family pride. I thought looking at photos on our phones was the safer bet.

Then I got asked about my political affiliations in their country - another topic I refused to engage in for a multitude of reasons. Although I was a bit uncomfortable in the twenty seconds between the gaze from the man in the row ahead of me till I brought out photos, at no point did I feel unsafe.

From a Westerner’s perspective, I felt I barely touched the tip of an iceberg to understand how much a Muslim woman faces in her country. From the traditional scarves loosely draped over each shoulder to hide the breasts as to the typical daily wear called a Salwar Kameez garment that looks like a long tunic, women are expected to be covered and compliant.

Any clothing that conceals cleavage or shows the curvature of the hips is considered vulgar by most. You'll see some women wearing jeans, but their shirts are usually long enough to cover their backside.

The members in class who were ready to meet the demands of the WAFW did so with astounding commitment. The progress they let me witness was as profound as it was innocent. Much like a child learning instills pride in any parent, these women became my daughters. Their accomplishments became victories that fulfilled me in a way that words cannot express.

There was little to no room for our curriculum until the women let go of some of the pain of their past. Then gradually, the emotional cups of each woman in the academy, regardless of how long they remained in the program, were overflowing. There's nothing like watching a woman hear something that sinks in.

One woman made a statement in class about a conversation she had with a person who supposedly "knew" what she meant, felt, or thought about a particular topic. It then occurred to me how often people make this same assumption because the person we're communicating with knows us well.

An insight unfolded for me, which I immediately brought into the lesson - for someone to know something, first, they must care. When a person cares enough about you, they make an effort to understand what you're talking about and will ask questions. From that understanding, a knowing develops. First and foremost, the person listening needs to care.

We often laughed at the response a person who doesn't care offers when you ask them something, the rapid response of, "yeah, yeah,

yeah," is a sure sign they don't care. Or at least they don't care as much as you do.

Another thing that surprised me in the third month of participation in the WAFW was how much these women trusted each other. When asking for a show of hands reflecting how many knew without a doubt that the other women in the class had their backs, not one hand got raised. I was shocked. After all the progress made, it was peculiar. Come to find out; they still didn't trust themselves. Certainly not exclusive to Bangladesh.

Bengali women are no different than most other females on the planet when it comes to placing the concern for another's welfare over their own. I've seen women who were sick keep their pain to themselves because they thought their parents were already too stressed about other things. They didn't want to be a burden.

Women of most ages in most cultures take ridicule and judgment personally. Some shake it off quicker than others. Some dwell in unworthiness for decades and find it hard to believe they are capable, deserve fair treatment and recognition. When you watch a woman step into realizing her worth as a human being and as a leader, it's like seeing a woman give birth. A miracle unfolds in front of you, and you express gratitude for the privilege.

The attachments I have to Bangladesh, and the women in the WAFW run deep. They are my daughters in every sense but biological. Love runs thicker than blood.

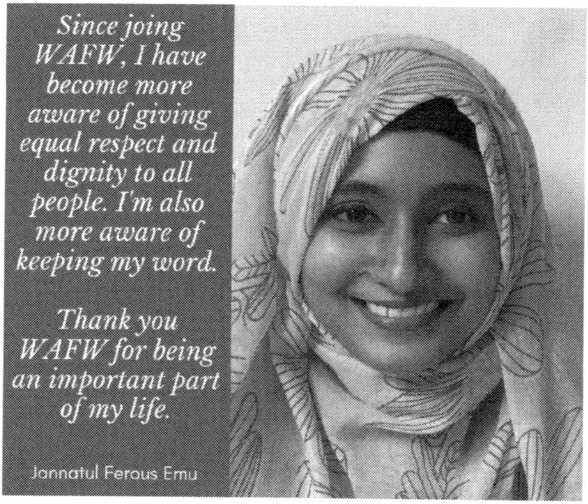

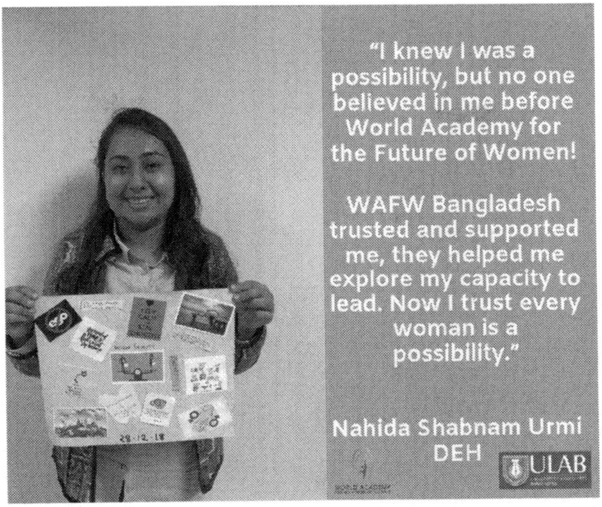
"I knew I was a possibility, but no one believed in me before World Academy for the Future of Women!
WAFW Bangladesh trusted and supported me, they helped me explore my capacity to lead. Now I trust every woman is a possibility."
Nahida Shabnam Urmi
DEH
ULAB

"World Academy for the Future of Women has widened my vision about the true meaning of service and helping others globally."
Khadija Rubaiyat Tasmia DEH
WORLD ACADEMY
ULAB

I can describe the difference I feel from WAFW in one word, enlightening.
Kazi Afia Tasnim

MAHFUZA KAZI
Are you an introvert? Facing challenges? Getting bullied? Then maybe it's time time to join WAFW.
I am more energized, inspired and capable of doing more than I believed possible!

I used to see problems everywhere. Since I've become a member of WAFW I look for solutions rather than counting my problems.
TANZILA JOTY

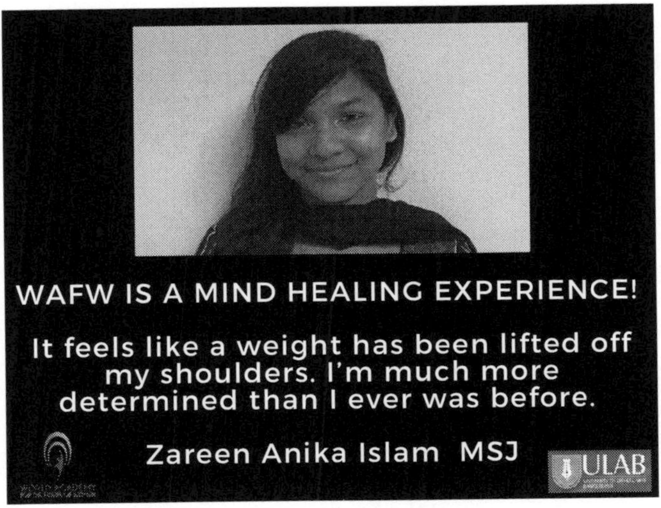
WAFW IS A MIND HEALING EXPERIENCE!
It feels like a weight has been lifted off my shoulders. I'm much more determined than I ever was before.
Zareen Anika Islam MSJ
ULAB

"When you do nothing, you feel overwhelmed and powerless. But when you get involved, you feel the sense of hope and accomplishment that comes from knowing you are working to make things better."

- Pauline R. Kezer

Chapter 12

Why Does Feeling Safe Matter?

What was the most significant thing you recall about reading this book? Perhaps the irony of what you take is not about how you help others feel safe, but the realization of how safe you feel in your relationships.

For some feeling safe is having what many consider the basics in life:

- A job.
- A roof overhead.
- A reliable vehicle.
- A friend, lover or spouse.
- Health insurance.
- Money.

When you think about it, four of these five things are void of emotional depth, with a lover or spouse potentially falling into the same category.

Maybe you've been too busy surviving to worry about feeling safe, and now you want to ponder the concept. Much like the love languages earlier mentioned, once you know what helps you feel safe, you see the pattern of how you attempt to make others feel protected. You may be on point, or off base.

For me, creating space for emotional intimacy regardless of how I feel, is critical. It took a couple of years to build this type of relationship with my husband. In the beginning, I was the one too afraid to let my guard down. I was perfectly content in self-sufficiency. Thankfully he was patient.

A practice Wasaka and I developed is such an intimate experience; it's more fulfilling than physical intimacy. We refer to is as, "Diving in." It's also the quickest way I know to tell how comfortable someone is with you requires no words, nor does it take long. You'll need to conduct this exercise with an open heart and a pure intent.

Gaze into another person's eyes. The longer you hold the gaze, the more you trust one another. For Wasaka and I this has transformed into a complex exchange of spirit, mind, and energy that we can each feel physically. It takes time to attain such a level of intimacy, but when both people are committed, it can get achieved quicker.

A lot of people have trouble doing this exercise. There's a distinct feeling of transparency and vulnerability that triggers discomfort and causes one of you to break the gaze out of fear, shame or unworthiness. When you can see with your heart, and look through the lens of unconditional love and appreciation for the journey of another human being, it's one of the most beautiful things you'll ever experience.

A skill I've honed over the years that I reserve mostly for clients is channeling a gaze from someone they've lost. Through my eyes, I become who they want to see and convey a message they most desire to receive from their loved one. There's no ego involved, I don't always know who they see in my eyes, and there's no attachment to the message. It's another way of holding space for a person.

In the beginning, when you practice "Diving in" it can feel like a contest about who blinks first or who can withhold laughter the longest. Laughter is a mechanism to disguise a multitude of things from fear to uncertainty to pain. Have you ever heard someone say windows are the eyes to the soul? Or express a concern that someone will see right through you? It's rare to feel immediately comfortable and allow anyone "in" and risk getting "seen."

Before you begin eye gazing it's vital to check your intent and know why you want to do this exercise. If the result is about serving you instead of another, proceed with caution. I do it to convey love more than to receive it.

If you're ready to begin the next phase of your development on purpose, please read the eight suggestions below a few times. If any of the questions trigger you to respond negatively or fearfully, ask why. Beginning any journey of self-discovery requires first and foremost for you to know where you want to go. But before you create your plan, you have to see where you are without judgment. Avoiding the judgmental trap of comparison is a MUST! You are not your parents. What looks like an ideal situation from the outside is probably not as it appears.

Beware of false realities on social media; everyone wants to portray the warm and fuzzy, the "I've arrived at success" persona. Although some folks are posting more transparent segments of their life, this self-exploration is best done alone or with the assistance of someone you trust.

Here are some suggestions if you want to improve the way you show up to support the people you care for:

1. Take the Love Language quiz https://www.5lovelanguages.com/quizzes/

2. Identify up to three people you want to deepen your relationship with and mutually grow.

3. Figure out how much time each week you're willing to dedicate to growing the skill of helping people feel safe and schedule small blocks of time you will commit to keeping.

4. Commit to taking responsibility for what you feel, how you interpret information from others, and how you choose to act or react as a result.

5. Reach out to the people you want to work with, tell them about your project. Ask people how safe they feel with you. How can you help those who trust you, feel safer?

6. Remind yourself this is a journey of doing things differently, not better or worse. Be gentle on you when you default to old behaviors. Pick yourself back up and keep going.

7. Being human is a practice, not a perfect. It will take some time to develop skills, and when you attain what you want, you'll be in a different head and heart space. You may begin to realize behavior in others that are no longer acceptable. Remember the attention you needed to place on transitioning to a new way of being. It took recognition, desire, and determination. Avoid the temptation to blame those not ready to begin their journey. Limit expectations to yourself.

8. Consider how you can measure your progress. One easy way is to determine the thoughts, words or actions you most want to transform. Pay attention and note how many

times an hour, day, or week (not all three, pick one) you think, speak, or do something to gauge your starting point. Then based on the metric you choose, make notes throughout the day or week to see if the number reduces. Don't be surprised by what you measure. It's common to achieve success then have an off day or week. By noting your progress, you become more aware of the behavior. Remember, there's no room for judgment; this is an observation.

Do what you can to avoid the temptation of delaying. It was essential to make as clear as possible the options for moving forward. Whatever unpleasant complications in life you're experiencing, they are of your creation based on the choices you've made, the things you've said or withheld, and the treatment you've tolerated. I'm not judging; I'm bringing attention to what I've realized in my life and seen in many of my clients.

A quote that always makes me smile from the founder of WAFW, Jerrie Ueberle came from her husband, Jack. It reminds me of how I am the only one responsible for whatever I'm stuck in:

"What an interesting problem you've created for yourself."

I can't help but smile when I hear Jerrie say it, or when I see the expressions of those, I share the statement with - people laugh but sometimes laughter is a defense mechanism.

Another way I love to record my daily progress is micro-journaling. What once began with colorful notebooks transformed to smartphone notes when I started traveling more as the journal became too cumbersome. Now each night before I go to sleep I note fifteen things in less than five minutes:

- Five things that I'm grateful for or appreciate.
- Five things that brought me joy.
- Five things I deserve an "atta girl" for.

Gratitude is an exceptional awareness to bring into your life, you begin to take fewer things for granted and realize how much you have. When you can eventually be grateful for the most challenging experiences, you'll have turned a corner.

Notice the statement of things that brought joy versus making me happy. It's a deliberate play on words not to turn the responsibility of experiencing happiness over to someone else. We so often hear people claim, "you made me so happy" when it was a choice to experience joy. The most delightful thing can happen, but if you're not willing to feel the joy, it won't happen.

Lastly, the "atta girl" is about recognizing accomplishments regardless of the size. On challenging days when I have no energy or am struggling with a health issue, getting out of bed qualifies! On the other end of the spectrum, acknowledging a success builds my confidence especially when I venture into new territory.

The influence of a seemingly mundane ritual can change the way you sleep. Ending your day on a high note does wonders for the quality of rest because you practice positivity. The more you appreciate internal victories, the more you'll recognize the progress in others.

Thank you for your support by purchasing this book. All proceeds help me continue to influence change around the world. Knowing why I make money has changed the way I attract wealth. In receiving I can give more.

If you're inspired to know more about WAFW, go to www.wafw.org.

If you're interested in hosting a book discussion, workshop or retreat about any of the insights you've read, please go to https://www.surveymonkey.com/r/FBZH598

Here's to celebrating the possibilities when each of us realized what we want to feel safe and when we hold space for others to feel safe. We. Become. Unstoppable.

"The path to our destination is not always a straight one. We go down the wrong road, we get lost, we turn back. Maybe it doesn't matter which road we embark on. Maybe what matters is that we embark."

- Barbara Hall

About The Author

International Leadership Trainer, Spiritual Consultant, and Four-Time Author, Leslie Karen Hammond is a personal transformation expert who's created spaces for women to feel safe, peaceful and powerful for 20 years. She consistently takes empowered action to live her purpose. Leslie's calling is to inspire women globally to trust in self so they find the courage to inspire others regardless of their age. Leadership has no age boundary. Every woman is capable of influencing long lasting change.

Her specialty is helping women who serve or feel the calling to help others, get clear on what they will no longer tolerate. In turn women develop self-respect, learn to feel safe, find their voice and advocate for what they believe.

Leslie's clients experience significant breakthroughs throughout every aspect of their lives. She is a master at teaching women how to trust themselves, feel they belong wherever they want to be and how to be more empathetic without taking on the energy of others.

Every dollar she makes funds her continued research of the suppression of women in developing countries and their transformation to create a more equitable, harmonious world. Her exposure to women in Asia is just the beginning. Revealing how a woman's courage inspires generations to come has never been more critical than at this moment. Global Wisdom got created to ensure the uplifting and empowerment of women worldwide.

For more information about working with Leslie, where she is speaking, or following her travels, check her website:

www.LeslieKarenHammond.com or follow her on social media.

Healing Through Your Story

Healing Through Your Story

Leslie Karen Hammond

Stories Impact

@ConfidenceBldr

Leslie Karen Hammond

Global Wisdom

Made in the USA
Middletown, DE
08 July 2022

68696933R00128